RALPH MATHEKGA

THE ANC's LAST DECADE

*How the decline of the party
will transform South Africa*

Tafelberg

To my two children,
Mashiko and Gopakilwe

Tafelberg
An imprint of NB Publishers, a Division of Media24 Boeke (Pty) Ltd
40 Heerengracht, Cape Town
www.tafelberg.com

Text © Ralph Mathekga (2021)

All rights reserved.
No part of this book may be reproduced or transmitted in any form
or by any electronic or mechanical means, including photocopying
and recording, or by any information storage or retrieval system,
without written permission from the publisher.

Cover design: Nudge Studio
Book design: Nazli Jacobs
Editing: Angela Voges
Proofreading: Alfred LeMaitre
Index: Sanet le Roux

Printed and bound by CTP Printers, Cape Town

First edition, first impression 2021

ISBN: 978-0-624-09203-2
Epub: 978-0-624-09204-9

Contents

Foreword by Stephen Grootes		1
Prologue		5
ONE	The fatal flaw in the giant's DNA	7
TWO	Walking between raindrops	18
THREE	Bulletproof at the ballot box	38
FOUR	State Capture Central	49
FIVE	Paralysed by an economic war	62
SIX	A breach in the giant's defences	76
SEVEN	The stumbling opposition	91
EIGHT	How much time does the ANC have left?	104
NINE	The morning after Election Day 2029	118
TEN	The coalition conundrum	132
ELEVEN	Is there a soft spot in the ANC's hard core?	143
TWELVE	The homeless middle class	153
THIRTEEN	The Rubicon conference	162
FOURTEEN	Pretenders to the crown	170
FIFTEEN	Ramaphosa's legacy	181
SIXTEEN	South Africa's giant slayers	190
SEVENTEEN	A strange new world	199
Acknowledgements		209
Index		211
About the author		217

Foreword
by Stephen Grootes

———◆———

It is no secret that we are living through interesting times, through a period of change in which the old is dying and, as the overused quotation goes, the new cannot yet be born.

There are so many dynamics that are changing our society, and the world, at this juncture. And so many of them contradict one another.

The rise of identity politics, to remove the dominance of arguments about left/right economic policy, has come as a surprise to many. But it is coming at a time when racial and economic inequality is more of a burning issue both here and around the world than at almost any other time in the past 70 years. It is both a symptom and a driver of the move towards identity being the dominant issue.

Our politics is still dominated by the ANC, and here the movement is divided, with dynamics pushing and pulling in different ways. President Cyril Ramaphosa appears to be in charge, but faces challenges from people such as the now-suspended Ace Magashule and others in the RET faction. David Mabuza is one of the quietest deputy presidents of our recent past, but must have ambitions of his own. Paul Mashatile is making interesting interventions as ANC treasurer-general.

And in the middle of it all is us. The voters and citizens and people who live in our fair land are caught between the anger and frustration of protests and outrage and Twitter, and the political peace that we have sought for so long.

How will it all pan out? It's hard to know. But it may be important to avoid being surprised.

There is no better guide to both our present and our future than Ralph Mathekga. It takes real skill first to understand what is happening in our society, and then to explain it to others.

There are so many questions about how the ANC will behave in the future. What will happen if Ramaphosa loses power? What will happen if he gains more power? What will happen if it is someone else?

The opposition parties, and opposition politics as a whole, are in a state of flux. Helen Zille appears to be running part of the DA, which is losing support it had won previously.

The EFF is hard to penetrate analytically but remains a major force in our national narrative. Herman Mashaba, Mmusi Maimane and others are hoping to make their mark.

While the politicians fight, squabble and tweet, the lights go out on a regular basis, sewage flows through the streets and economic reform seems far off. Which leaves so many remaining so poor, with no prospect of a job and regular income.

In some ways, we may be coming very close to a fork in the road – between a brighter path of reform and a future even more difficult than our present.

There are no simple answers to how it will play out. But there are trends that you can examine, and dynamics that point to possible outcomes. Ralph is more qualified to do this than just about anyone.

Of course, it is not just about the parties.

One of the most under-examined dynamics in our society is how power continues to democratise, how it is flowing away from the centre and to the provinces and regions. There may now be places in our country where the identity of your mayor, or the party governing your council, may have more of a bearing on your life than any national government policy does.

Foreword

This is surely going to upset the power balance in our politics, and scramble things even more.

However, the most important person in the country is not the president, or the secretary-general, or the leader of the EFF. It is you, the voter, the citizen.

Our politics is supposed to benefit you.

For that to happen, our politics must also lead to economic growth, a situation that gives you hope that the lives of your children will be richer and better than yours has been.

Our future will require a careful analysis of our problems.

It will also require bravery.

You will find both in this book. Ralph has demonstrated that he is not scared to tell the truth, whether he is speaking directly to an arrogant politician or to a disappointed voter.

Sometimes, people claim that our democracy is under threat. Instead, the opposite may be happening. People who claim to be in charge often show us how weak they are, how they cannot achieve their stated aims.

This is not always a good thing.

There are many reasons to hope. You will be reminded about them in this book, about the power of ordinary citizens and how important voters really are.

The rate of change is likely to pick up. And, as this book demonstrates, it is likely to involve a weakening of the ANC, to the point where it loses national power.

If you want to know what that process looks like, read on.

Prologue

On 8 January 1912, a colossus was born that would one day tower over the South African political landscape. During a long and arduous struggle stretching over 82 years, it carried the hopes of the country's downtrodden majority, before finally vanquishing their oppressive rulers.

Once in power itself, the giant was untouchable. It knew the people it had liberated would never forsake it and that it would rule 'until Jesus came'.

It brooked no opposition, and swatted away its would-be challengers as if they were irritating insects. It did not help that many of these challengers seemed to have the lifespan of a mayfly. They kept on fighting among themselves – sometimes with more vigour than that with which they battled the giant.

At first glance, the giant looked invincible. But the close observer would notice that its belly was starting to get a bit rounded, as if it had been gorging itself on the fat of the land. During its years of struggle, it had been lean, supple and quick on its feet – constantly on the move. But now, as it approached three decades in power, the comfortable life was beginning to slow it down. Its muscles were starting to atrophy, even as it retained its huge bulk.

Internally, its health was in even worse shape. Its arteries were clogged and its habit of overeating had increased its risk of cancer.

Psychologically, it sometimes looked as if the giant was torn in two, with duelling alter egos battling it out. Some days, its more disciplined personality from its glory days would come to the fore. But then, just as quickly, it could turn into a gluttonous and greedy dictator.

Through sheer size alone the giant was still unbeatable, but the seeds of its destruction had been sown. Exactly when this destruction would come was still unclear, but one thing was certain: If the colossus were to fall, it would be an almighty crash that would reverberate across the land.

ONE

The fatal flaw in the giant's DNA

The African National Congress (ANC) wears the label of Africa's oldest liberation movement with pride. During its 109-year history, the party has seen two world wars, the rise and fall of communism, and now also a global pandemic.

Ironically, it might be precisely this long history – the glorious past of which the organisation is so proud – that sowed the seeds of its potential destruction. Perhaps the very traits that had helped the giant to vanquish an evil and unjust system are the ones bedevilling it now.

Let us unearth some of the important clues contained in the ANC's rich history, clues that help us understand how the ANC arrived at its current position: a party seemingly at war with itself, battling to rein in corrupt cadres and trying to wrest control of the state away from special interests – both within and without.

The ANC likes to portray itself as a party of the people where decisions are made from the ground up. In this telling, the party is but a vehicle for the will of the masses, whose decisions and wishes bubble almost magically to the surface. Nowhere is this more apparent than when the time for internal ANC elections comes around. Potential leadership contenders are loath to declare point-blank that they want the top job, preferring to intimate that they will only throw their hat in the ring if it is the 'the will of the branches'. It is a fairly transparent charade, but it is telling that most contenders feel compelled to go along with it.

When the ANC celebrated its centenary in Mangaung in 2012, the party's pride in its history was on full display. The city of Bloemfontein was draped in black, green and yellow, with huge cooling towers featuring larger-than-life portraits of previous ANC presidents. The ANC's dominance of the Mangaung landscape that weekend mirrored the iron grip the party had on South Africa's politics. In the previous national election, held in 2009, it had lost a bit of ground compared to its high-water mark of 69,7 per cent support in the 2004 election, but it was still sitting pretty. The party had received 65,9 per cent of the vote in 2009, just a hair's breadth away from the two thirds needed to make changes to the Constitution. There was no Economic Freedom Fighters (EFF) to worry about, yet, and its nearest rival, the Democratic Alliance (DA), was a distant second: at 16,66 per cent, nearly 50 percentage points behind the ANC electoral juggernaut.

But the ANC's dominance was about more than just numerical superiority. Just as powerful was the grip the party had on the country's political imagination. Most South Africans, including political commentators and even opposition politicians, simply could not fathom a future in which the ANC was not in charge.

As the party celebrated its 100th birthday in Mangaung, it appeared to be untouchable. The celebrations showed a party confident of the future, but perhaps even more secure in its past. Those attending the event were left in no doubt about the ANC's view of its history: rather than a mere political party, it was a mass movement, South Africa's liberator and the only true voice of the people. There was, of course, a large measure of truth to this portrayal, but it also obscured some uncomfortable facts about the direction the organisation had taken during its long history – a path that has now brought it to a moral crossroads.

Although the ANC was destined to develop into an organisation that would grip the imagination of the masses, it was largely members of the African elite who gathered in the Waaihoek Wesleyan Church (a school at the time) in Bloemfontein on 8 January 1912 to form what was initially called the South African Native National Congress. Its founding president was the distinguished publisher, author and educator, John Langalibalele Dube. After attending a private school in the USA, Dube returned home, where he founded a girls' school and started the isiZulu newspaper *Ilanga*. Other founding members included Pixley ka Isaka Seme, one of the first black lawyers in South Africa, the noted intellectual Sol Plaatje and various traditional and religious leaders.

The organisation's primary goal was the liberation of South Africa's native black people from the subjugation and discrimination that they faced in the country of their birth.

The bulk of the ANC's 109-year history was spent in the pursuit of this founding mission, with the party labouring for 82 years before finally reaching its promised land. After more than eight decades as a liberation movement, it finally became the party of government in 1994, a position it has held for 27 years.

It was a case of the dog catching the car. In the decades that followed its ascension to power, it became clear that the ANC, although a great liberation movement, was a poor governing party. Was it a case of the ANC betraying its legacy, as many have claimed, or was this outcome the almost inevitable consequence of its history?

In his article 'The ANC in exile',[1] historian Stephen Ellis provides valuable insight into a critical phase of the ANC's history: the three decades from 1960 to 1990 when the organisation was banned by the apartheid government. It was during those years in exile that the ANC organisational culture was cemented. During this period, as several historians have noted, the organisation gradually shifted

---

1   Ellis, S. 1991. The ANC in exile. *African Affairs*, 90: 439-447.

from a broadly democratic decision-making process to one in which the party elites held sway over the masses. Open debates and dissent were stifled.[2]

ANC leaders steeped in this culture of centralisation would play an integral role in the negotiations with the apartheid government and, eventually, in South Africa's first democratic government. As such, understanding the ANC in exile is key to understanding the party's later struggles in government.

The ANC's shift to a more autocratic decision-making process is by no means unique among liberation movements. Faced with external pressures in the midst of a heated war for survival and freedom, these groups often veer away from their founding principles. The phenomenon is well captured by Berkley Eddins: 'Liberation movements, while they may have quite correctly and admirably as their goals the seeking of equity and equitable access to the exercise of power and decision-making, nevertheless may, in fastening those goals, be illiberal in their larger implications and dimensions.'[3]

When these liberation movements eventually assume power, they often have difficulty operating in a plural democratic system.

In the specific case of the ANC, the party adopted the principle of 'democratic centralism' while in exile. This system was cemented at the ANC's Morogoro Conference in Tanzania in 1969, held after nine difficult years in exile, which included failed military campaigns. Before the conference, the leadership of the party in exile faced open mutiny and challenges to its authority, precipitating the shift towards a more autocratic decision-making process.

---

2   For more on how the ANC functioned in exile, particularly on how the party dealt with dissent, see also Melber, H. (ed.) 2003. *The Limits to Liberation in Southern Africa*. Pretoria: HSRC Press.
3   Eddins, B.B. 1972. Liberalism and liberation. *Social Theory and Practice*, 2(1): 99–112, p. 110.

As Ellis explains: 'The Morogoro conference ... sealed the [Communist] Party's supremacy and the principle of democratic centralism within the ANC, and hence destroyed the prospect of real debate on certain fundamental subjects.'[4]

Even as liberation movements shift towards more centralised decision-making systems, they still place great emphasis on the collective, or the majority, as the only source of legitimacy for policy decisions – whether or not the masses were really that influential in the process. The collective good is prioritised over the needs of the individual.

This focus on the collective means that liberation movements are often ill-suited for the demands of a liberal democratic system of governance, with its emphasis on the rights of the individual.

In this regard, the ANC is no exception. A feature of the party's reign has been tension between its project of transformation and the liberal democratic ideals on which South Africa's Constitution is based. Since it came to power in 1994, the ANC has pursued a transformative agenda – aimed at ensuring equality for black South Africans after centuries of discrimination. This agenda includes policies such as black economic empowerment (BEE), affirmative action and, more recently, the land reform policy. In addressing deep-seated structural inequality and poverty, it is an agenda that sometimes necessitates that the rights of a specific individual be subjugated to the rights of a specific group within society. While this is necessary for righting the wrongs of the past, it can create a schism between the government's policies and the liberal principle of individual equality.

The problem lies not so much with this almost unavoidable tension, but rather with the ANC's reaction to criticism of these policies

---

4   Ellis, S. 1991. The ANC in exile. *African Affairs*, 90: 439-447, p. 444.

and to criticism in general. The lack of a strong internal democratic culture in the ANC – in part a remnant of its years in exile – means that policies are not questioned and interrogated thoroughly. Once something has been established as party dogma, for example BEE, it becomes almost untouchable. Even merely asking whether there might be a better way of implementing that specific policy can meet with stiff resistance.

The ANC has become impervious to criticism, which leads to substandard policy outcomes when constructive suggestions are swept from the table because they do not align with party orthodoxy.

Additionally, the ANC's conflation of party and state means that even well-meaning critics are sometimes branded as unpatriotic. Open and robust debates are regarded as a threat to the pursuit of national interests, resulting in political leaders making decisions without meaningful consultation with the wider public. As noted above, this culture of centralisation is deeply ingrained in the ANC from its years in exile. Controversially, some authors point to the influence of the South African Communist Party (SACP) on the ANC following the Morogoro Conference. Ellis, for example, blames the SACP for 'infiltrating' the ANC and instilling a Stalinist model of leadership. It decrees that leaders are not to be challenged, as this would undermine the discipline of the organisation.

Political organisations without a pluralistic and participatory leadership culture usually lack an internal correction mechanism – especially when they find themselves excessively dominated by elite groups. This domination is seldom admitted, with the organisation in question preferring to hide behind the veneer of mass participation. The elites convince themselves that they are the embodiment of the collective will. This general principle is especially true in the case of the ANC. One diagnosis of the ANC's struggles in government is that the party elites have diverted the organisation from the very people it should be representing.

'No, no, no!' one can almost hear the ANC spin doctors say. 'We are not dominated by elites. Every decision flows from the *branches*.'

It is indeed theoretically true that the ANC branches do wield influence over decision-making in the party. But in practice it is the National Executive Committee (NEC) and the so-called Top Six who make the bulk of the decisions. Additionally, the extent to which branch members, especially those in poor, rural areas, can be beholden to those with their hands on the levers of power and patronage should not be underestimated.

In modern democratic systems, it is taken for granted that individual leaders take individual responsibility for government decisions. 'The buck stops here,' as former US president Harry Truman famously declared. In the ANC, the principle of individual accountability is much more elusive. The concept of 'the collective' is often wielded as a shield to evade personal responsibility. The 'collective' sometimes refers to the grassroots members of the ANC, whom the leaders claim to be representing, but also to the top leadership of the party, for example the NEC or the Top Six. In government, ministers are fond of claiming that they are merely implementing decisions that the Cabinet arrived at as a 'collective'. Whichever way it is (mis)used, the concept of 'collective responsibility' provides cover for individual leaders whenever unpopular decisions are made. It mystifies citizens and voters, who are unsure about how the party arrived at a particular decision, often taken behind the closed doors of an NEC meeting, and it leads to public anger when there is no one to hold accountable. In summary, the ANC's organisational culture is not aligned with the principle of individual accountability demanded by citizens from leaders and codified in the legal instruments of a modern democracy.

This culture is another legacy of the ANC's years in exile. It is difficult for a liberation movement to defeat an oppressive regime when the role of the individual is prioritised over collective solidarity. So, in many ways, the ANC's approach to leadership during its struggle years was a pragmatic choice – perhaps even a necessity if collective emancipation of the country's black majority was to be achieved.

However, the ANC's collectivist roots were always destined to become entangled with the principles of a modern liberal democracy, which prioritises the rights of the individual and does not put much stock in the concept of collective justice or collective guilt.

Some senior ANC leaders have at last begun to confront the reality that the ANC's struggle history, while in many respects admirable, has not always been useful in preparing the party to lead a pluralist democratic society. Rather, the very traits that had helped it survive a brutally oppressive regime had set the ANC on an institutional path that would one day burden it in government.

But, for all its challenges as a ruling party, the ANC is still a behemoth at the ballot box. When one party dominates the landscape to this extent, it fosters interest group politics centred around the party's internal machinations. The competition between the different factions – or interest-groups – in the party are often more intense than the fights against weak opposition parties at the ballot box. And the prize for winning the internal battle in a dominant party can be huge, as the Jacob Zuma era showed in South Africa.

Across southern Africa, erstwhile liberation parties are still firmly in the driving seat. Opposition parties in the SADC region are often institutionally marginalised and have found it extraordinarily difficult to wrest power from incumbent liberation parties, with the 2020 Malawian elections being a notable exception. The institutional culture entrenched in these liberation movements – an intolerance towards dissent and opposition – is replicated in government institutions.

As the last liberation movement to oversee a transition to democracy in southern Africa, the ANC had a golden opportunity to learn from the experience of other liberation parties in the region. Instead, it has plunged headlong into some of the same traps. The fostering of the aforementioned interest-group politics – as opposed to a democracy based on overarching national goals – ranks prime among them. The ANC's failure to mediate the conflict between its warring factions has turned the party into a battleground for competing interest groups, undermining the pursuit of a pluralist, participatory democracy. The resulting bargaining between interest groups has radicalised South African politics to the point of stagnation and complete dysfunction.

Had the ANC heeded the history of other liberation parties and avoided the pitfalls of democratic centralism, the party would have held its leaders accountable as individuals for the decisions they have made in government. Instead, it has allowed its leaders to hide behind the concept of collective responsibility.

Since 1994, the ANC's best moments have come when it has pursued common goals agreed upon through a process of national consensus, as opposed to a political agenda driven through majoritarianism. This unifying, non-racial approach was exemplified by the presidency of Nelson Mandela. Sadly, it has been all too rare since.

In many ways, the ANC's ambitious aims to transform the country are laudable, However, it falters in the implementation phase. The ongoing internal battle between President Cyril Ramaphosa and the faction once commandeered by former president Jacob Zuma is no longer just a conflict over so-called rent-seeking and the distribution of patronage through the state; there is also deep division about how to re-energise the ANC's fading transformation agenda for the country, and how to renew the party itself.

On these matters, the ANC has postulated at great length but without much progress in implementation. At the heart of the problem lie two conflicting philosophies regarding how the party ought to lead. On the one hand, there are those who maintain that the ANC should renew itself by emphasising collective discipline, whereby all members must yield to the organisation. To put it simply, this faction demands loyalty to the organisation at all costs. On the other hand, there is another group that believes that leaders should first and foremost be accountable to those who vote for them instead of being loyal to an organisation. In this view, direct accountability to the people is the pinnacle of participatory democracy.[5]

The collapse of accountability in the public service in South Africa under ANC rule coincided with the party's intensification of its transformation project, particularly the BEE programme. As noted, the overarching aims of these programmes are laudable and necessary. However, by casting every aspect of these policies as a non-negotiable that is not subject to critical evaluation by anyone, the ANC created an environment that could be exploited by unscrupulous actors, from both inside and outside the party. Under the guise of BEE, one could get away with almost anything. Anyone questioning the manner in which it was being implemented at the height of the Zuma and Gupta years ran the risk of being branded an anti-transformational heretic. The lack of a strong internal democratic culture meant the party could not be easily rescued from the clutches of those who captured it from within.

While the looting of public resources hitherto undoubtedly reached its zenith in the Zuma era, it is too easy an explanation to attribute this grim period in the party's history solely to the moral failings of one man and his cronies. The reasons for the ANC's

---

5 Mathekga, R. 2006. Participatory democracy and the challenge of inclusion: The case of local government structures in post apartheid South Africa. *Colombia Internacional*, 63: 88–107.

malaise run much deeper than that. The party's history left it ill-equipped to govern a liberal democracy with accountability and transparency. Put more bluntly, the ANC in its current state and South Africa's Constitution are just not a very good fit. And the battle for the soul of the party is still far from over.

As the 109-year-old giant stands at the moral crossroads, gazing into the future, the ghosts of the past are still howling in its ears.

TWO
Walking between raindrops

President Cyril Ramaphosa entered the Union Buildings on a tightrope.

Having won the leadership of the ANC by the slimmest of margins at Nasrec in December 2017, he inherited a party torn in two. The deep divisions in the ANC hang like a shadow over Ramaphosa's presidency. They have influenced both the substance of his policies and the speed at which he has been able to implement them. Ramaphosa's measured approach has come in for stinging criticism from some commentators, who like to paint him as a spineless ditherer who shies away from tough decisions.

Is Ramaphosa man or mouse? Or does the truth lie somewhere in between?

To begin to answer this question, one should look at the circumstances in which he came to power. To win the ANC presidency, Ramaphosa had to defeat Nkosazana Dlamini-Zuma, the anointed candidate of the Zuma faction. Dlamini-Zuma may not see herself as a proxy for this faction and we do not know the extent to which she would have done its bidding had she been elected. The fact remains, however, that she had the full-throated support of the Zumaists, who at the time held huge power in the ANC and in government, having taken control of almost every state institution. It was clear that the Zuma faction would not go down without an almighty fight – and the final margin of Ramaphosa's victory bears testimony to this. He defeated Dlamini-Zuma by only 179 votes out of 4 501 cast. Another indication of how close Ramaphosa came to disaster is that Ace Magashule, a staunch Zumaist, won the race for secretary-general against Senzo Mchunu, the preferred candidate of the reformers. Only a late deal with then Mpumalanga premier David Mabuza ensured Ramaphosa's victory.

Although Ramaphosa's faction won the plum prize of the presidency, it was not a total victory. Only two other members who were clearly aligned with him won positions in the Top Six of the NEC: Gwede Mantashe (national chairman), who won by 149 votes, and Paul Mashatile (treasurer-general), who won by 339. The other jobs went to Magashule (secretary-general, 24 votes), Mabuza (deputy president, 379 votes) and Jessie Duarte (deputy secretary-general, 261 votes). The narrow margins of victory revealed how evenly the party was split. The Zuma faction had lost one or two battles, but it was nowhere near vanquished.

The ANC of which Ramaphosa was now the leader was a broken party, undermined by factions competing for power and influence in government. In February 2018, three months after his victory at Nasrec, he also became the leader of a broken government, when Zuma was finally forced out. The full extent of the brokenness would later be revealed in gruesome detail at the Judicial Commission of Inquiry into Allegations of State Capture (the Zondo Commission), which had been tasked with investigating how government had been infiltrated by interest groups such as the Gupta family and their associates.

Virtually no government department or state institution escaped the state capture years unscathed. The ANC's dysfunction became South Africa's dysfunction.

The culture of impunity and disrespect for party rules prevalent within the ANC spilled over to the public sector, in part due to the policy of cadre deployment. The resulting institutional decay led to rampant corruption and the collapse of service delivery.

The ANC's failure to sanction senior members accused of impropriety was replicated in government and state institutions, turning watchdogs such as Parliament into puppy dogs.

As leader of both the ANC and the government, Ramaphosa straddles two worlds. Success in the party increases the chances for success in government. However, coming short in the party does not necessarily mean the president will also fail in implementing his agenda in government. Ramaphosa has at times managed to keep the two worlds sufficiently apart for him to manage the conflicts that arise when the party and government are not completely aligned on policy matters.

After the Nasrec conference, which laid bare the dividing lines in the ANC, Ramaphosa vowed to unite the party and deal with the factionalism that had pitted leaders against one another. Despite these public pronouncements, Ramaphosa was probably enough of a realist to know that the ANC in its current state could never be fully united.

Anyone expecting that he would charge in following his narrow Nasrec victory and start cleaning the Augean stables would have been disappointed. Even though his campaign was based on organisational renewal of the ANC and the restoration of integrity, compromised members of the ANC were not immediately sidelined. Rather, he tried to keep the tent as big as possible, even as he quietly and carefully began manoeuvring against those most tainted by the state capture years. A full three and a half years after his victory at Nasrec, Ramaphosa's slow poison finally began to have an effect, with the suspension of Magashule, his main internal rival, in May 2021.[6]

Characteristically, Ramaphosa did not move against Magashule

---

[6] Hunter, Q. & Etheridge, J. 2021. Ace Magashule suspends Ramaphosa – but ANC says it is not possible. News24, 5 May 2021. https://www.news24.com/news24/SouthAfrica/News/ace-magashule-suspends-ramaphosa-but-anc-says-it-is-not-possible-20210505. Last accessed 17/05/2021.

directly, even though the secretary-general had become the de facto leader of the Zuma faction, now also known as the RET (radical economic transformation) faction. In the events leading up to Magashule's suspension, Ramaphosa avoided criticising his rival in public. Similarly, he has steered clear of overt criticism of Zuma, just as he did while serving as his deputy president.

Instead of confronting Magashule head-on, Ramaphosa and his allies pushed a general resolution through the ANC's NEC, mandating that any party leader criminally charged with corruption or other serious crimes must 'step aside'. As Magashule is facing a raft of charges relating to the asbestos scandal in the Free State, he was squarely in the resolution's firing line.

In typical fashion, Ramaphosa still allowed his rival a chance to save face. Firstly, the wording of the resolution euphemistically called on the affected leaders to 'step aside', as opposed to an outright suspension. Secondly, Magashule was allowed 30 days to make a show of 'consulting' with 'party elders' about the best course of action. With these measures, Ramaphosa tried to open the door as wide as possible for Magashule to make his exit voluntarily.

The secretary-general slammed it shut.

After he refused to step aside willingly, the ANC's National Working Committee authorised his suspension. In a last gambit – indicative of both his desperation and his animosity towards Ramaphosa – Magashule tried to use his powers as secretary-general to suspend the president. The quixotic effort had little practical effect – Magashule was no longer secretary-general and, even if he was, he could not suspend the party leader unilaterally – but it did blow up the façade of 'ANC unity' once and for all. Not that too many people were buying the story any more in the first place.

As the factional battles have raged over the past few years, the warring parties have also drifted further apart on policy issues, adopting an adversarial tone that sometimes makes it difficult to believe that they are members of the same party. As Stanley Mathabatha, the premier of Limpopo, put it at an NEC meeting following Magashule's suspension: 'Do we still have an organisation called African National Congress, or do you have two or three groupings or factions who all claim to be representing the organisation claiming to be the ANC?'[7]

Rather than grabbing this bitterly divided organisation by the scruff of the neck, Ramaphosa has walked between the raindrops. The president shies away from direct and overt skirmishes with any one faction. He draws on his negotiating skills, honed during his union years, to work within the warring factions in an attempt to gain the space necessary to implement key policies and attain some measure of organisational renewal.

The appointment of Ramaphosa's new Cabinet after the 2019 general elections was emblematic of his compromising approach.

In terms of ANC tradition, it is the deployment committee of the ANC that decides on government appointments. However, the president usually has great leeway in choosing a Cabinet that fits in with his governing agenda, or at the very least does not undermine it.

In Ramaphosa's first Cabinet, the factional lines were clearly drawn, with the two main interest groups in the party almost equally represented.

It is notable, however, that Ramaphosa identified a few key ministries where the appointment of his allies would be non-negotiable. One was the Cabinet's financial cluster, which would be tasked with fulfilling one of the government's central policy aims: rebuilding the

---

7   Du Plessis, C. 2021. ANC NEC meeting characterised by deep 'hate' between members. News24, 8 May 2021. https://www.news24.com/news24/southafrica/news/anc-nec-meeting-characterised-by-deep-hate-between-members-20210508. Last accessed 17/05/2021.

economy and utilising the bridges that the president had built during his career in the private sector.

With former Reserve Bank governor Tito Mboweni heading the Treasury, and Pravin Gordhan as Minister of Public Enterprises, Ramaphosa gained full control over the economic cluster. Gordhan, especially, is a trusted Ramaphosa ally, who played a vital role in stabilising the Treasury after Zuma's shock firing of Nhlanhla Nene and the short-lived appointment of Des van Rooyen as Minister of Finance in 2015. In addition to his two stints as Minister of Finance, Gordhan was also a highly respected commissioner of the South African Revenue Service (SARS). At the Department of Public Enterprises, his is the Herculean task of trying to rescue state-owned behemoths such as South African Airways (SAA) and Eskom.

To install his allies in the key economic posts, Ramaphosa had to compromise when it came to deployments in the security cluster. These positions were given to members who can hold their own in the ANC and do not align themselves explicitly with any one faction. For example, Ayanda Dlodlo, who was appointed Minister of State Security, is an MK veteran who cut her teeth in exile and can move between factions if she wants to. Likewise, Nosiviwe Mapisa-Nqakula (Minister of Defence and Military Veterans) is a senior member with enough standing not to have to nail her colours to the mast of a particular interest group. The police ministry was handed to former SAPS chief Bheki Cele, another senior member who can hold his own in the party. None of the three ministers in the security cluster were traditional allies of Ramaphosa, but nor could they be associated with the Zuma faction.

Ramaphosa's approach to the security cluster stands in marked contrast to that of his predecessor. Control of these ministries was a key part of Zuma's strategy to keep himself and his allies out of legal trouble. It extended beyond the Cabinet to institutions such as the National Prosecuting Authority (NPA). Some of these appointments so clearly served the president's personal interests that the courts intervened. In 2009, for example, Zuma appointed his ally Advocate Menzi Simelane to head the NPA, an appointment that was later ruled irrational upon legal review.

Stability in Zuma's world relied on control of the security cluster, while Ramaphosa seems happy to leave it in the hands of more neutral actors.

In other departments Zuma allies were able to hold on to Cabinet positions, for example Thulas Nxesi (Minister of Employment and Labour), who famously defended the Nkandla 'fire pool', and Maite Nkoana-Mashabane (Minister of Women, Youth and Persons with Disabilities), who lost out to Paul Mashatile for the job of treasurer-general at Nasrec.

The retention of the Zuma allies disappointed outside observers who had been hoping for a more wholesale change. 'It is quite clear that this Cabinet is not President Ramaphosa's first choice,' remarked the seasoned economist Iraj Abedian.[8] The *Daily Maverick* ran a story with the headline 'Horse-trading and compromise: Ramaphosa's realpolitik Cabinet'.[9]

The appointment of the Cabinet was a chance for Ramaphosa to draw a line in the sand, and make it clear to the party that deploying individuals who are compromised or have a history of non-performance would no longer be tolerated. In a well-functioning

---

8   Cape Talk. 2019. It is quite clear this is not Ramaphosa's first choice. Cape Talk, 28 November 2019. http://www.capetalk.co.za/articles/368330/it-is-quite-clear-that-this-cabinet-is-not-president-ramaphosa-s-first-choice. Last accessed 14/05/2021.

9   Merten, M. 2019. Horse trading and compromise: Ramaphosa's realpolitik Cabinet. Daily Maverick, 30 May 2019. https://www.dailymaverick.co.za/article/2019-05-30-horse-trading-and-compromises-ramaphosas-realpolitik-cabinet/. Last accessed 14/05/2021.

democracy, Cabinet appointments are based on merit rather than loyalty to a specific faction. This sounds like a fairly simple principle but can be a challenge even in mature democracies.

It was clearly a bridge too far for Ramaphosa, who sensed that his position in the party was not strong enough to push for a wholesale Cabinet makeover. It would set the tone for the rest of his presidency.

The pursuit of greater unity in the ANC has also stalled, despite Ramaphosa's regular statements about the destructive power of factionalism. The ANC branches have weakened and young people are growing increasingly disgruntled with the party, with some finding refuge in the EFF.

The ANC Youth League (ANCYL), which has been losing influence since the expulsion of Julius Malema from the organisation, is yet to be stabilised after being used as a pawn in factional battles during the Zuma years. The National Youth Task Team, which was appointed by the NEC to stabilise the ANCYL, does not have much to show for its work, with some members of the league questioning its constitutionality and continued failure to resolve the problem.[10]

The NEC itself is bitterly divided, and takes a painfully long time to reach the tough decisions necessary to overhaul the party.

During the state capture era, some internal structures of the party, such as the Integrity Commission, also proved to be ineffective when they did not have the backing of the NEC. The Integrity Commission was set up after a resolution at the ANC's Mangaung conference in 2012. It was supposed to 'deal with public officials,

---

10 Tandwa, L. 2020. Disband unconstitutional task team now – high-ranking ANCYL members. News24, 27 August 2020. https://www.news24.com/news24/southafrica/news/disband-unconstitutional-task-team-now-high-ranking-ancyl-members-20200827. Last accessed 14/05/2021.

leaders and members of the ANC who face damaging allegations of improper conduct'.[11]

The founding members of the commission, which was officially established in 2013, included party luminaries such as Rivonia trialists Andrew Mlangeni (its first chairman) and Ahmed Kathrada, as well as former Speaker of Parliament Dr Frene Ginwala. Their mandate was straightforward: investigate and recommend sanctions against members of the party who have been implicated in or found guilty of crimes such as corruption.

Despite these high ideals, the Integrity Commission quickly gained a reputation as a toothless watchdog, with senior leaders flouting its recommendations with impunity. For example, the commission had recommended that Zuma step down as president a full five years before his actual departure, according to testimony at the Zondo Commission by Gwede Mantashe, secretary-general during the state capture years.

Ramaphosa has been vocal about corruption and poor discipline in the party, but hesitant to wage all-out war over these issues. Given the state of the party he inherited, he enjoyed a honeymoon period, dubbed 'Ramaphoria', where he was given the benefit of the doubt. But at some point it was no longer enough merely to point a finger at the Zuma legacy.

As impatience with the slow pace of change in the ANC grew, some progress was at last made with the suspension of Magashule, as well as those of other key members of the RET faction, such as Supra Mahumapelo. The former premier of the North West was suspended for a period of five years by the ANC structures in the

---

11 News24. 2013. ANC establishes integrity committee. News24, 18 May 2013. https://www.news24.com/News24/ANC-establishes-integrity-committee-20130318. Last accessed 14/05/2021.

province after he arranged a rally to compete with an official rally organised by the provincial leadership in December 2020.[12]

Nonetheless, the large number of party deployees who continue to serve in top positions despite credible evidence of their incompetence or malfeasance speaks to the weakness of the ANC's disciplinary processes. There is seldom a consequence for failing to execute the party's mandate in government.

For all the difficulty Ramaphosa has had in coralling the wild horse of the ANC, he has been able to move more quickly in government, notably in beefing up critical institutions that were almost completely hollowed out during the state capture years – the National Prosecuting Authority and the South African Revenue Service, for example. It was as if Ramaphosa, having realised that the task of renewing the ANC would be more challenging and time-consuming, poured more of his immediate energy and efforts into shaping government policies and institutions. It would, of course, be impossible to negate the ANC's influence completely. But Ramaphosa has worked around the ANC's policy edicts – which are often more in the form of general demands than a coherent set of proposed regulations – and managed to limit the impact of the party's contentious deployment strategy on his government.

Government institutions, when they are functioning properly, are held together by a complex network of bureaucracy, allowing for the institutions to have some level of resistance to undue political influence. Because of the ANC's policy of deploying its cadres in every nook and cranny of government, South Africa's bureaucracy has been politicised, with party leaders openly influencing

---

12 Letshwiti-Jones, P. 2021. ANC suspends Supra Mahumapelo for five years. News24, 28 April 2021. https://www.news24.com/news24/southafrica/news/just-in-anc-suspends-supra-mahumapelo-for-five-years-20210428. Last accessed 17/05/21.

appointments in key state institutions. This trend started long before the state capture years, but it gathered pace under Zuma. He may not have invented cadre deployment, but he seemingly did perfect it.

A public sector that prioritises party loyalty over competence gradually loses the ability to deliver services, before collapsing completely. When this happens, citizens – especially the poor and vulnerable – bear the brunt of the pain.

Another toxic feature of the public service under ANC rule has been the tendency of senior officials to do business with government entities – on a national, local and municipal level. This clear conflict of interest has led to the establishment of wide-ranging patronage networks, created and nurtured by ANC leaders.[13] Once established, they are exceedingly difficult to root out, due to their lucrative nature.

When a new minister is appointed, it is common practice for the senior management of the department to be purged. The new boss then brings in the cronies from his previous stop. This revolving-door style of management destabilises departments and leads to the loss of institutional memory and skills, exacerbating the service delivery crisis in the public sector.

The challenge for Ramaphosa and the reformers in the ANC is that the tentacles of the party's patronage networks stretched deep into the heart of almost every government institution during the Zuma years. One can turf out the Gupta family, but in many ways they were just the tip of the iceberg. One can clean out a key institution such as the NPA, but what about the hundreds of municipalities where smaller-scale but no less damaging looting is taking place?

---

13 Pillay, I., Pikie, Y. & Kesavan, S. 2020. Corruption and a dysfunctional state: the interface between political leaders and public administration. *Daily Maverick*, 21 January 2020. https://www.dailymaverick.co.za/article/2021-01-21-corruption-and-a-dysfunctional-state-the-interface-between-political-leaders-and-public-administration/. Last accessed 14/05/2021.

As Mcebisi Jonas, former Deputy Minister of Finance, put it: 'You will find a mini Gupta in every town.'[14]

Given the state of the public service that Ramaphosa inherited, it was probably always unrealistic to expect him – or anyone else – to turn everything around at once. Rather, Ramaphosa's strategy was to identify the most critical institutions and target them for immediate intervention. For many, this was not enough, and the president has faced a barrage of criticism for not moving faster with his reform programme – in both government and the ANC. This is probably not surprising. In a society increasingly focused on instant gratification, we are all conditioned to expect results much more quickly than we were a few decades ago. These modern-day expectations do not always align well with the ANC's institutional culture, which stretches back for more than a century.

Ramaphosa probably deserves more credit for rebuilding some of the pillars on which our democracy rests. Prime among these is the South African Revenue Service, which provides the fuel to keep the engine of government running. A dysfunctional SARS means an underfunded and dysfunctional government.

Under commissioners such as Pravin Gordhan, SARS had become a world-class tax-collection agency. For many years, it was the crown jewel in South Africa's public sector: a well-functioning organisation in a sea of mediocrity and incompetence.

For the first five years of Zuma's presidency, SARS somehow managed to avoid the marauding gang of looters and hijackers masquerading as a government. But it could not escape capture indefinitely. When SARS finally fell, it fell hard.

---

14 Malan, P. 2018. 'n Guptatjie in elke dorp. *Rapport*, 17 June 2018. https://www.netwerk24.com/Nuus/Misdaad/n-guptatjie-in-elke-dorp-20180616. Last accessed 17/05/2021.

In 2014, Zuma appointed one of his old struggle comrades, Tom Moyane, as SARS commissioner. Moyane, a former prisons boss, had no previous experience in tax collection.

Moyane immediately set about muzzling SARS's investigative bloodhounds; rumour had it that they were sniffing too close to the president and his allies. After Moyane began his purge, a culture of fear and suspicion paralysed the once effective organisation. An exodus of skills followed.

SARS was just one of many institutions to be gutted as part of the state capture project, but a collapse there could unleash a domino effect threatening every aspect of government.

If Ramaphosa's economic policies were to have any chance of success, he would need to shore up SARS. Recognising that the revenue service was the bedrock of the financial cluster, Ramaphosa moved quickly after taking over the presidency in February 2018.

Moyane did not last much more than a month under the new administration. Following Moyane's suspension by Ramaphosa, Mark Kingon was appointed as acting commissioner. Kingon, who had been with the tax agency since its inception, almost immediately brought a sense of stability to SARS.

In March 2019, Edward Kieswetter, another SARS veteran, became the full-time commissioner. Kieswetter had left SARS in 2014 as Zuma tightened his grip on the institution. He has built on the work done by Kingon, restoring integrity and competence at the revenue service and cementing one of the success stories of Ramaphosa's presidency.

The National Treasury is another institution in which Ramaphosa has been able to undo some of the worst damage of the state capture era. The Treasury was the scene of some of the hardest-fought battles during the latter part of the Zuma years. Nothing was more valuable to the Gupta family than getting their hands on the national purse. Jonas sensationally claimed that the Gupta brothers offered him R600 million to do their bidding at Treasury – an eye-popping amount, but a bargain for the keys to the state's vault.

During the presidencies of Nelson Mandela and Thabo Mbeki, the Treasury established a reputation as a stable and efficient government department, led by a respected Minister of Finance in Trevor Manuel, who would hold the job for thirteen years.

The financial cluster was on a particularly solid footing during the Mbeki era, with Manuel at Treasury, Gordhan at SARS and Mboweni at the Reserve Bank. They had the trust of the markets and, for the most part, the trust of the ANC's members. All three institutions were well aligned with Mbeki's agenda of fiscal consolidation and budget rationalisation. The Medium Term Expenditure Framework had strengthened South Africa's fiscal position.

All of the economic gains of this era would eventually be squandered during the Zuma years, even though the Treasury was initially able to resist attempts at capture. Under Gordhan, who took over as Minister of Finance from Manuel, and under Nhlanhla Nene, who succeeded Gordhan, the ministry was able to retain a large measure of independence. But, just like SARS, it was not able to hold out forever.

On 9 December 2015, the dam wall burst and Treasury's defences were breached. In a dramatic late-night announcement Zuma fired Nene and replaced him with a hitherto unknown ANC backbencher, Des van Rooyen. It was clear that this was no ordinary Cabinet reshuffle – Nene was the only minister being replaced. As the rand and the markets plunged, it soon became clear that Nene had been fired because he had crossed Dudu Myeni, Zuma's confidante at South African Airways. Faced with economic disaster, Zuma was backed into a corner. Ramaphosa, with the support of business heavyweights such as Patrice Motsepe, told the president in no uncertain terms that Van Rooyen would have to go. Until that point, Ramaphosa, ever the cautious party man, had served loyally as Zuma's deputy president, seldom upsetting the applecart, even as he had a front-row view of the excesses of the state capture years. The president was forced into a humiliating climbdown and had to bring his old nemesis, Gordhan, back for a second stint as finance minister – just days after firing Nene.

In 2017, Zuma finally managed to get one of his allies, Malusi Gigaba, into the Treasury's top job, even though it was rumoured that his first choice had been former Eskom boss Brian Molefe. Gigaba, once a rising star in the party, with a penchant for high living, was at this stage widely regarded as one of the 'Gupta ministers'. The Zuma wing of the party was now in full control of both the Treasury and the taxman.

As with SARS, Ramaphosa moved quickly to re-establish control of Treasury after Zuma was forced out. Less than two weeks after Ramaphosa had assumed the presidency, Gigaba was gone, to be replaced by Nene, the man Zuma had fired. Under the leadership of Nene and later Mboweni, the Treasury regained its former independence – in no small measure thanks to Ramaphosa's decisive action and strong appointments.

The Department of Public Enterprises was another vital cog in the economic mechanism. When Ramaphosa took over, it was faced with a myriad challenges. The state-owned enterprises (SOEs) under its wing were in dire straits. Eskom was struggling to keep the lights on while racking up massive debts. SAA was heading for a crash landing with serious concerns about its viability as a going concern.

Run properly, SOEs can be a force for good in an economy by driving investment in public infrastructure and creating jobs in line with the government's strategic goals. Under the ANC's stewardship, however, SOEs have been a drain on the fiscus, with multibillion-rand state rescue packages handed out like candy. In turn, the SOEs doled out enormous salaries to their top officials and fat contracts to well-connected suppliers.

As with SARS and the Treasury, Ramaphosa moved quickly to regain control over this critical department. The minister, Lynne Brown, was shifted aside and replaced with Gordhan. Truth be told, this portfolio was always going to be a hospital pass, but Gordhan accepted the challenge.

Ramaphosa's efforts to right the ship on SOEs have been markedly less successful than his interventions at SARS and Treasury. For the most part, the SOEs are still basket cases. Eskom is still struggling to keep the lights on and SAA's future – even with a 51 per cent stake in the hands of a strategic equity partner – remains uncertain – to name but two examples.

The one bright spot is that the looting of public resources and the dispensing of patronage have become less rampant – even as the SOEs continue to struggle operationally. At Eskom, for example, CEO André de Ruyter is cracking down on exorbitant deals struck during the state capture years, ranging from toilet paper to coal contracts.

So, at least, there is less open theft going on. The Zuma era set the bar low enough that this has to be chalked up as a win for Ramaphosa.

Another key institution gutted during the Zuma years was the National Prosecuting Authority, one of many factors allowing corruption to run rampant. Control of the criminal justice system was a central plank of the Zuma strategy, with only the judiciary managing to retain full independence. As political interference increased, the NPA became beset with factional infighting, with talented and seasoned prosecutors driven out.

To get the organisation back on track, Ramaphosa appointed an independent external panel to make recommendations about the appointment of a new director of public prosecutions.[15] This unprecedented step brought transparency to a process that had been marred by political interference since the Mbeki presidency. It culminated in the appointment of Advocate Shamila Batohi, a respected prosecutor with nearly a decade's worth of experience at the International Criminal Court.

Like the president, Batohi has been accused of moving too slowly, particularly in pursuing and prosecuting state capture cases, but there is no sense that she is guided by political rather than legal motives. Batohi has pointed to the hollowing out of the NPA during the Zuma era as one of the reasons for prosecutions stalling. Nonetheless, there has been some progress in state capture cases, with the arrest of Magashule in the Free State asbestos case and that of several other officials in the Estina dairy matter.

To deal with Zuma-allied senior prosecutors, Ramaphosa set up a commission of inquiry headed by retired judge Yvonne Mokgoro in 2019. She was tasked with investigating the fitness to hold office of axed deputy NPA boss Nomgcobo Jiba and former Special Director of Public Prosecutions Lawrence Mrwebi. Her findings paved the way for Ramaphosa to strengthen Batohi's hand by replacing them with uncompromised prosecutors.

It was vintage Ramaphosa – and typical of the strategy he has used to attain some measure of success in the rebuilding of key institutions. Rather than pulling out the sharp knife immediately, he often prefers to appoint an independent panel or commission to investigate a particular official or matter. The president handpicks the members of the commission himself. After its investigations, the

---

15 Sehloho, M. 2018. President Ramaphosa appoints panel to assist in new NPA boss hire. 702.co.za, 10 October 2018. http://www.702.co.za/articles/322462/president-ramaphosa-appoints-panel-to-assist-in-new-npa-boss-hire. Last accessed 14/05/21

commission issues a recommendation that more often than not leaves Ramaphosa with little choice but to act against the accused. This modus operandi means he has no blood on his hands, and it has the added benefit of acting as a safeguard against possible legal action by the fired official. As the ANC is notoriously slow in acting against its compromised and incompetent deployees in government, this method provides Ramaphosa with a much more efficient way to enforce accountability.

The president employed the same tactic to deal with the SARS matter. He established the Nugent Commission of Inquiry into Tax Administration and Governance by SARS in 2018. This paved the way for Ramaphosa to officially fire Moyane, eight months after suspending him.

The Public Investment Corporation (PIC) and its CEO, Dan Matjila, also received the Ramaphosa treatment. The PIC, charged with managing the retirement assets of public services, is another institution in the financial cluster that was used as a kitty by ANC comrades and their networks. To deal with this matter, Ramaphosa appointed a commission of inquiry led by Judge Lex Mpati in 2018.[16] Its findings allowed the president to clean out the board and remove Matjila. The commission found that there was 'substantive impropriety'[17] at the state-owned asset manager.

By opting to use the independent inquiries, Ramaphosa sidestepped the usual bureaucratic processes that are fraught with ANC

---

16 Savides, M. 2018. Ramaphosa sets up commission of enquiry into the PIC. *TimesLIVE*, 17 October 2018. https://www.timeslive.co.za/politics/2018-10-17-ramaphosa-sets-up-commission-of-inquiry-into-the-pic/. Last accessed 14/05/21.

17 Magubane, K., Khumalo, S., Van der Merwe, M & Omarjee, L. 2020. PIC commission of enquiry report released, finds board was 'rubber stamp' for Matjila. *News24*, 12 March 2020. https://www.news24.com/fin24/companies/financial-services/pic-commission-of-inquiry-report-released-finds-board-was-rubber-stamp-for-matjila-20200312. Last accessed 14/05/21.

factional politics. Even as he has sometimes been stymied with his renewal agenda in the party, he has nonetheless found a way to achieve relative success in government. 'One must distinguish between what the state is doing and what the ANC is doing or not doing,' wrote analyst JP Landman in his assessment of Ramaphosa.[18] 'He has clearly put the state on a new trajectory. It is important that the ANC now follows suit.'

With this last sentence, Landman makes an important point. Even though Ramaphosa has showed that it is possible to work around his own party on policy matters, this strategy has its limitations. At some point, the tension between government action and ANC policy will reach breaking point.

Ramaphosa still needs to bring his party along to craft a clear agenda for government. Tackling corruption and incompetence in key institutions is one thing, but it will be difficult for Ramaphosa to enact meaningful economic reform if the ANC is continuously left out of the policy dialogue.

Political realities, coupled with Ramaphosa's inborn caution, have left many disappointed with the pace of change, but the president has unquestionably managed to restore credibility to key parts of the public sector after years of despondency and helplessness under Zuma. Additionally, his boa constrictor approach to dealing with his internal foes has started to squeeze the RET faction – even though the Zumaists show no intention of going down without a fight.

Is the president sometimes too circumspect and not decisive enough? Perhaps.

On the other hand, he is a shrewd leader who has spent a lifetime

---

18 Landman, JP. 2020. Ramaphosa has put the state on a new trajectory, check his scorecard. News24, 18 August 2020. https://www.news24.com/fin24/Opinion/jp-landman-ramaphosa-has-put-the-state-on-a-new-trajectory-check-his-scorecard-20200818. Last accessed 14/05/21.

in the ANC and has an intimate knowledge of its inner workings. It is clearly his considered judgement that moving at a faster pace could jeopardise the reform project – both in party and government. Given how difficult it can be for outside observers to gain an understanding of the ANC's internal machinations, it would be imprudent simply to dismiss his concerns out of hand.

The stakes are high – and beneath the president's tightrope is a moat full of crocodiles.

THREE
Bulletproof at the ballot box

'Cry the betrayed country.'

It was hard to miss the huge billboard on the M1 highway in Johannesburg. The message was part of an advert for eNCA, South Africa's first 24-hour TV news network. During the height of the state capture period, the network gained a reputation for critical and independent journalism – at a time when one wouldn't find that on the TV screens of the SABC, and certainly not on GuptaTV, otherwise known as ANN7.

Despite some bad apples, South Africa by and large has a lively and robust media. With most law enforcement agencies under the effective control of the Zupta faction, journalists played a vital role in exposing the crimes of the state capture era. In my role as a political analyst, I speak to journalists on an almost daily basis about political and other developments. Just like other citizens, they are patriotic and want their country to succeed. So, when a respected news channel such as eNCA starts using terms like 'betrayal', I sit up and take notice.

Are things really that bad under the ANC government, or are we exaggerating?

In most democracies, it would be unusual for a party that trounced its nearest rival by 37 percentage points in free and fair elections to face such searing questions about its legitimacy to make decisions and govern. In the last general election, held in May 2019, the ANC secured 57,5 per cent of the national vote.[19] Although it was the first time since 1994 that ANC support dipped below 60 per cent, its share of the vote was still double that of its nearest rival, the DA (20,7 per cent).

By most measures, the ANC has a strong mandate from the voters. Yet, all indications are that it has a serious image problem. For many South Africans, the party has become synonymous with corruption. When the COVID-19 pandemic hit, necessitating public spending on personal protective equipment (PPE) and other measures, social media users were quick to predict that this would provide yet another opportunity for cadres to feed from the government trough. It did not take long for those fears to be realised.[20] The Special Investigating Unit found that R30,7 billion had been spent from April 2020 to November 2020 – R13 billion of which was under investigation. The state bought PPE at highly inflated prices, with a mark-up, sometimes, of as much as a 100 per cent.

President Cyril Ramaphosa himself took to his weekly newsletter to bemoan the looting: 'As scores of people became ill and many were dying, some people saw an opportunity to cash in . . . Individuals and entities with no experience in the manufacture, supply of distribution of critical medical supplies hastily set up companies. In some cases they were registered on national databases and received purchase orders. In others they weren't even registered but

---

19 Electoral Commission of South Africa. 2019. 2019 National and Provincial Elections. https://www.elections.org.za/NPEDashboard/app/dashboard.html. Last accessed 14/05/2021.
20 Heywood, M. 2021. The great PPE scandal: Masuku and SIU duke it out in high court. *Daily Maverick*, 21 January 2021. https://www.dailymaverick.co.za/article/2021-01-21-the-great-ppe-scandal-masuku-and-siu-duke-it-out-in-high-court/. Last accessed 14/05/2021.

profited nonetheless. This includes entities operating as a car-wash and a shisa nyama.'

The ANC's apparent image problems extend beyond social media, which is of course not representative of the electorate as a whole. In rural towns across the country, municipal services have collapsed, sparking service delivery protests when citizens' anger with their local politicians boils over.

In an Afrobarometer survey prior to the previous election, 60 per cent of respondents said they had no or little trust in the ANC. But when it comes time to vote, the giant pulls out its suit of armour from its glory days, reminds the people who it was who liberated them and promises better days ahead. Its foes can barely put a dent in its defences.

The disconnect between the ANC's support at the ballot box and its public image is one of the most vexing questions in South African politics. Perhaps a part of the answer lies in another data point in the same Afrobarometer survey. Even more unloved than the ANC are the opposition parties, with 70 per cent of respondents expressing no or little trust in them.

The ANC itself has no doubt about who to blame: the media. Senior ANC officials often accuse mainstream news organisations of misrepresenting the ANC's 'good story'[21] in their coverage. At its Mangaung conference in 2012, the party adopted the following resolution: 'Whereas weaknesses have been identified in government communications, the media continues to have a propensity to publish mainly negative news on government disregarding the good service delivery record of government. The media continues to dis-

---

21 Africa Check. 2014. Africa Check: Does the ANC have 'a good story to tell'? *Daily Maverick*, 25 April 2014. https://www.dailymaverick.co.za/article/2014-04-25-africa-check-does-the-anc-have-a-good-story-to-tell/. Last accessed 14/05/2021.

tort and ignore information provided by government in a transparent and accountable manner.'[22]

This sums up the ANC's view of the media: an irritant providing a distorted view of the party and its achievements.

In the past three decades, South Africa has experienced rapid democratisation and transformation as well as major economic and technological change. When this is coupled with unrealistic expectations about what democracy would bring, it is not surprising that disappointment and disenchantment with the system have set in. In many ways, it is an almost unavoidable part of South Africa's democratic consolidation.

Do the media, and South Africans in general, give the ANC too little credit for what has been achieved?

South Africa's democratic consolidation has been a mixed bag, with impressive progress in some areas, worrying reversals and stagnation in other areas, and prospects for improvement here and there.[23]

It is no secret that corruption is one of the major challenges facing the country, undermining the capacity of the state to deliver basic services to its citizens and poisoning the soul of the nation. No government institution, big or small, local or national, has been spared.

It is a cancer that has spread to every part of the giant's ageing body. A radical dose of chemotherapy would seem to be the only solution, but whether the party has the stomach for this is yet to be seen.

As local governments have been turned into feeding troughs, municipal services have collapsed. In extreme cases, ratepayers have

---

22 African National Congress (ANC). 2012. Resolution of the 53rd National Conference. https://www.sahistory.org.za/sites/default/files/resolutions53r.pdf. Last accessed 14/05/2021.
23 Mtlosa, K. 2014. The state of democratisation in South Africa: Blocked transitions, reversals, stagnation, progress and prospects. *Politikon*, 44(1): 5–26.

taken it upon themselves to keep the taps running and the potholes filled. In Koster and Swartruggens, for example, residents sued the ANC-run Kgetlengrivier Local Municipality to gain control of the local water and sewage works.

Some municipalities are unable to even pay monthly salaries. Once, a headline such as 'State runs out of cash, struggles to pay salaries' would have been unfathomable. Yet this was precisely the gist of a *City Press* article[24] detailing the extent of the financial problems at, among others, state-owned arms manufacturer Denel and rail operator Metrorail. The story also quoted the South African Municipal Workers' Union as saying that 30 of the country's 226 local municipalities were battling to pay salaries.

Corruption is an insidious foe: It takes a while for its effects to become visible. Strong institutions can withstand its effects if they have enough of a hard core of skilled and dedicated workers who can still keep the engine running. But when corruption and nepotism also lead to these workers being replaced by unqualified cadres, it is a poisonous brew.

A sustained attack orchestrated at state level will eventually overwhelm whatever natural resistance remains in government institutions. During the state capture years, South Africa's institutions were overrun by the Zupta faction. Once captured, the damage can take years to rebuild.

Some level of patronage in the procurement of goods and services in the public sector is almost unavoidable. If, for argument's sake, R10 of every R100 is stolen but R90 is still used to provide a service or maintain infrastructure, total collapse is prevented. Unfortunately, it seldom ends there. Once someone gets away with stealing R10, it becomes R20, then R30 . . . and so on.

---

24 Eybers, J. & Khumalo, J. 2019. State runs out of cash, struggles to pay salaries. *City Press*, 1 July 2019. https://www.news24.com/citypress/news/state-runs-out-of-cash-struggles-to-pay-salaries-20190701. Last accessed 14/05/2021.

A decade ago, South Africans were not always attuned to the link between their socioeconomic conditions and acts of corruption in the public service. That is changing as disgruntled citizens begin to connect the dots between their situations and poor decisions made in government. They realise that the pothole in their street might be caused by money being siphoned off the road maintenance budget.

When the lights go off because Eskom has not maintained its power-generation infrastructure, South Africans are quick to point a finger at the ANC government, which allowed the looting of public entities during the Zuma years.[25] Public indignation at the behaviour of the ANC in government is palpable, and some senior leaders, including Ramaphosa, have begun to share with South Africans their anger about their own party's role.

As trust in leaders is eroded, the country's youth grows more disaffected and disillusioned with politics. The latest research shows that '... young people are more comfortable engaging in other forms of activism, such as service delivery protests and protests at university campuses, which have become commonplace occurrences in South Africa'.[26]

Traditional political activities such as voting are increasingly being shunned. Prior to the 2019 election, Glen Mashinini, chairman of the Independent Electoral Commission (IEC), announced that only 16 per cent of young people aged 18–19 had registered to vote – a sharp decline from the 34 per cent prior to the 2014 elections. The

---

25 BBC. 2019. Eskom crisis: Why the lights keep going out in South Africa. BBC World News, 16 February 2019. https://www.bbc.com/news/world-africa-47232268. Last accessed 14/05/2021.

26 Tshuma, D. & Svaita, GT. 2019. Political fatalism and youth apathy in South Africa: Analysis of the 2019 General Election. *Conflict Trends*, 2019/03. https://www.accord.org.za/conflict-trends/political-fatalism-and-youth-apathy-in-south-africa/. Last accessed 14/05/2021.

number of 18 to 19-year-olds registered to vote was the lowest since the IEC started keeping track in 1999. Just under 400 000 were registered, compared to just over 600 000 in 2016.

The youth are no longer willing to engage with the political system; they only aim to disrupt it. This is the politics championed by the Economic Freedom Fighters. The aim is to disrupt the political system through informal mechanisms such as protests and picketing.[27]

When the executive branch of government is failing or captured, it falls to the legislative branch to exercise its constitutionally mandated oversight. Unfortunately, the ANC's culture of centralisation, which stretches back to its years in exile, has seen successive governments weaken Parliament's watchdog role. The situation reached its zenith during the state capture years. Time and again, ANC MPs chose party loyalty over their parliamentary oath.

'Parliament was sleepwalking for a long time,' admitted Sydney Mufamadi, a former Minister of Safety and Security, during his testimony before the Zondo Commission. His remarks were later echoed by Thandi Modise, former Speaker of the National Assembly. 'It is really regrettable that Parliament woke up when things were now really bad ... and for that we must apologise to the South African people,' she told Zondo.

Not only did Parliament fail to fulfil its role as watchdog, but some MPs allegedly became active parts of the state capture network themselves. Former ANC MP, Vincent Smith, has been criminally charged because of his ties to Bosasa, a company that received multi-billion-rand prison contracts from the state. Another ANC MP,

---

27 For an extensive discussion on politics of disruption, see Mathekga, R. 2018. *Ramaphosa's Turn*. Cape Town: Tafelberg.

Cedric Frolick, who chaired the parliamentary ad hoc committee on Nkandla, has also been accused of being on the Bosasa payroll. Both deny the allegations.

When safeguards such as parliamentary oversight fail in this manner, the political system cannot self-correct, further eroding the trust of young people and other citizens.

Even without this erosion of trust, South Africa already had a mountain to climb to establish a cohesive political system. History has shown that countries with a long history of conflict and deep divisions across racial and ethnic lines have to work extra hard to cultivate an inclusive and consensus-driven political culture.

When a conflict-riven history is combined with rapid societal change on several fronts, the result is political instability. Political scientist Samuel Huntington sums up the situation as follows:

> Political instability in Asia, Africa, and Latin America derives precisely from the failure to meet this condition: equality of political participation is growing much more rapidly than 'the art of associating together'. Social and economic change – urbanization, increases in literacy and education, industrialization, mass media expansion – extend political consciousness, multiply political demands, broaden political participation. These changes undermine traditional sources of political authority and traditional political institutions; they enormously complicate the problems of creating new bases of political association and new political institutions combining legitimacy and effectiveness. The rates of social mobilization and the expansion of political participation are high; the rates of political organization and institutionalization are low. The result is political instability and disorder. The primary

problem of politics is the lag in the development of political institutions behind social and economic change.[28]

Huntington's hypothesis implies that the ANC, even without its many shortcomings, would struggle to transform South Africa into a successful democratic society glued together by liberal values. Countries with a history such as ours present a challenge to liberal democracy. South Africa's economic and other ills cannot be solely blamed on the ANC; they are also an indication of the limitations of the liberal project when it comes to building nations that emerge from a history of conflict. In some instances, the adoption of liberal principles, such as reducing the role of the state in the provision of public goods and the privatisation of public entities, can open the door to corruption and patronage. Former Wits professor Tom Lodge has argued that the privatisation of some bulk services in the City of Johannesburg (done in the name of financial rationalisation) has paved the way for corruption.

But all is not doom and gloom, despite the sombre picture sketched by Huntington. Singapore and Malaysia have shown that postcolonial societies with a history of conflict are able to forge a development and political agenda upon which a strong and capable state grounded in democratic principles can be built.[29]

While the ANC cannot be blamed for the existence of structural inequalities in post-apartheid South Africa, the party's leaders can and should be held accountable for its uninspired economic leader-

---

28 Huntington, SP. 1968. *Political Power in Changing Societies*. New Haven, CT: Yale University Press, p. 5.
29 White, NJ. 2017. The settlement of decolonisation and post-colonial economic development: Indonesia, Malaysia, and Singapore compared. *Bijdragen tot de Taal-, Land- en Volkenkunde*, 173(2/3): 208–241.

ship. For too long their focus has been on their own wallets, rather than on the wallets of their voters.

When a party is as dominant electorally as the ANC, it is easy for us all – from citizens to political analysts – to become obsessed with its internal politics and shortcomings. Media outlets magnify the minutiae and machinations of the party, while glossing over news and proposals from other political parties and groupings. It is time to break free from this obsession and start looking beyond the ANC for solutions. To be fixated on the party and its shortcomings is a collective failure of imagination and perpetuates the idea that it is only the ANC that determines our destiny.

The party certainly sees itself as indispensable. With public anger at revelations of corruption growing, ANC acting secretary-general Jessie Duarte confidently remarked that 'South Africa without the ANC could result in civil war'.[30]

Duarte's statement chimes with Jacob Zuma's infamous declaration that the party would rule 'until Jesus comes back'.

The ANC's failure to live up to its idealistic mandate is often couched in the terms of a political tragedy, the 'betrayal' of a nation by a party. There is sometimes an almost religious tone to the coverage, just as there was an almost religious tone to the coverage of former President Nelson Mandela – although its thrust was naturally very different. The nostalgia for the ANC's glory years is captured in the frequent calls for the organisation to self-correct and enter a journey of renewal and rebirth.

The sense of disappointment with the ANC is perhaps also exacerbated by unrealistic expectations of what a political party can

---

30 Mavuso, S. 2021. SA without the ANC could result in civil war, says Duarte. IOL, 4 January 2021. https://www.iol.co.za/news/politics/sa-without-anc-could-result-in-civil-war-says-duarte-e34c9fdb-a3e4-4bd5-acf9-4640b8c03748. Last accessed 14/05/2021.

achieve through public policy. In such a scenario, moderate failure could appear more tragic than is actually the case. We become consumed with the ANC's leadership, instead of focusing on strengthening and protecting institutions against undue political influence, regardless of whether a 'good' or 'bad' faction is in charge of the party at a particular moment.

A political party that loses its way is not a reason for national grief. It is a reason to look at alternatives. The problem becomes tragic only if one thinks there is some sort of moral covenant that exists between the party and the liberated nation. The ANC is decidedly not the only vehicle through which the morality of South Africa's politics can be preserved. Our political discourse should reflect this reality. It is time to shift away from the endless ruminating about how the ANC can be 'fixed' or 'healed' from within and broaden our thinking.

If we allow the giant to block out the sun, nothing will thrive in its shadow.

FOUR
State Capture Central

Once, they were household names synonymous with excellence. Now, they are bywords for failure, dysfunction and corruption.

Eskom.

SAA.

Transnet.

Denel.

Together, they have the power to cripple a country – either through the massive debt burden they have placed on the state or by failing to provide vital basic services.

South Africa's state-owned enterprises are hopelessly adrift, caught in a perfect storm, and – except for SAA – the the ruling ANC appears to have no long-term plan to bring them back from the brink. As this book was making its way to the printers, Gordhan announced that Cabinet had agreed to sell a 51 per cent stake of SAA to a strategic equity partner.

The history of the SOEs stretches back to the apartheid years. Each was created to provide a service regarded as vital and strategic by the state: electricity generation (Eskom), rail, port and pipeline services (Transnet), arms manufacturing (Denel) and aviation (South African Airways).

Eskom and Transnet, in particular, play crucial roles in the functioning of the economy. Load shedding has given us a worrying glimpse of a life without electricity, while Transnet's transport arteries provide the lifeblood for the economy. In its heyday, Denel played a key role in positioning South Africa as one of the leading arms manufacturers in the world. Eskom's electricity generation capacity was such that South Africa could extend services to neighbouring countries.

SOEs have been used strategically to support South Africa's industrialisation through the provision of critical services. However, in the past ten years, governance at SOEs has collapsed as corruption has run rampant. Some are no longer able to fulfil basic functions, leaving a gaping hole in South Africa's development strategy.

The logic behind the formation of SOEs is sound and, in the beginning, they lived up to expectations. They provide services that would usually not be initiated by the private sector because of the capital demands and the risk involved. Private companies usually shy away from projects that offer uncertain returns but demand extremely high capital investment. If a service is needed by society and its provision is seen as strategic for the development and wellbeing of the nation, the state should provide it.

Although SOEs were conceived to fill the gaps left by the private sector, this does not mean that government cannot, later in the process of development, allow the private sector to play a role. There is no good reason why the state should permanently retain full control of SOEs.

The problems at South Africa's SOEs didn't start with Jacob Zuma's presidency, but their position did worsen significantly during his term. In many respects, the SOEs were State Capture Central. Special interests within and outside the ANC, working in cahoots, took them over one by one, corrupting their core mission from serving the public to serving the interests of an elite group of party officials and businessmen.

The Zondo Commission has heard how Zuma interfered with the running of SAA by installing his allies in key positions at the airline, including Dudu Myeni as board chair. What followed were years of rampant mismanagement, with decisions made to serve the patronage networks flowing through the ANC. The Eskom story is the same and has also been laid bare at the Zondo Commission. The Gupta family and their political associates exploited lucrative coal contracts to bleed the electricity provider dry.

The result is that Eskom and SAA, perennially indebted and running at a loss, have become the single biggest threat to the country's fiscal future. Eskom alone owes nearly R500 billion, of which R330 billion is guaranteed by the state, while SAA has received multiple multibillion-rand rescue packages.

The SOE crisis was also underlined when the state military technology firm Denel announced in May 2020 that it did not have the cash to pay salaries for the month.

When Cyril Ramaphosa returned to politics, serving as Zuma's deputy from 2014, one of his main assignments was to 'stabilise' the SOEs. It was during those years that the rot at the SOEs became apparent to the public, with regular power outages revealing the level of financial mismanagement and destruction of capacity that was underway at Eskom.

Ramaphosa's image as a successful businessman who did not countenance corruption sparked hopes that the SOEs could be turned around. Some also felt that his involvement signalled a possible move towards greater privatisation in an attempt to improve services and alleviate the burden on the fiscus. In the end, the deputy president had precious little to show for his efforts. To this date, the ANC does not appear to have a coordinated, long-term strategy for the SOEs. It appears that the party is simply too divided to rethink the strategic importance of SOEs in the economic system. It is much easier to gather everyone under the banner of fighting corruption in the SOEs and freeing them from the patronage networks. Laudable and necessary as that is, it is not a substitute for a long-term strategy for the role of SOEs in our development plan.

The reasons for the malaise affecting our SOEs run deeper than just corruption. In many ways, corruption is a symptom of a larger problem: the location of SOEs in the current political structure. Are these enterprises optimally placed to evolve with the country's other institutions as part of our democratic consolidation? Does full state control of these enterprises hinder or help them to achieve their core aims?

These are the underlying questions that need to be addressed, even as the attempts to root out corruption continue at SOEs. That there is a consensus across the nation about the detrimental impact of corruption on SOEs and the broader public service[31] does not mean that there is an agreement that the SOEs should be freed from corruption by privatising them, although ongoing developments at SAA at the time when this book went to print indicate that the ANC government is open to strategic partnerships. Proponents of privatisation point out that the SOEs are being run inefficiently and not in accordance with market principles. By lessening the pull of political influence, they believe, these entities could be placed on a different trajectory.

There is also the question of partial versus full privatisation. In this regard, the ANC seems to have adopted a policy of having its cake and eating it. It has maintained that SOEs should remain in the hands of government, but the private sector should be encouraged to invest in them.

Since the Nasrec conference in December 2017, the ANC has reiterated its intention for SOEs in a resolution by the party's National Executive Committee in December 2019. The resolution was adopted after SAA was placed under business rescue in the same month when the airline's cash crunch finally reached breaking point after more than a decade of government bailouts. The outbreak of the

---

31 For an extensive discussion about this, see Mathekga, R. 2018. *Ramaphosa's Turn*. Cape Town: Tafelberg.

COVID-19 pandemic in February 2020 would further cloud the airline's future. In response, the ANC came out with a position that, despite the collapse of governance and the poor performance plaguing the SOEs, the party would not support privatisation of these entities. The ANC announced: 'The NEC agreed that the challenges faced by our SOEs require a comprehensive approach, as well as bold and creative solutions that give effects to the resolution of the national conference which states "the main purpose of SOEs is to operationalise the broad socio-economic development plans of government".'[32]

This boils down to the ANC saying that the SOEs are still seen as strategic assets through which the party aims to pursue its transformation agenda, so they should remain under government control. Sociologist Roger Southall lucidly summarises the ANC's attitude towards the SOEs: 'While offering the ANC considerable economic leverage, the parastatals were also to serve as a major platform for black managers aligned with the ANC subsequently to move into high positions within the private sector.'[33]

The ANC's aim of using the SOEs to drive its economic transformation agenda not only failed but also opened the enterprises to capture by special interests. Despite all this, the party has maintained that government control of SOEs is strategic in advancing the transformation agenda.

Ramaphosa's administration is caught in the middle of the ANC's policy morass, undermining his ability to reposition the SOEs to

---

32 Nyathi, M. 2018. ANC says 'no privatisation of SOEs' but open to investments. *City Press*, 11 December 2019. https://www.news24.com/citypress/news/anc-says-no-privatisation-of-soes-but-open-to-investments-20191211. Last accessed 14/05/2021.

33 Southall, R. 2014. Democracy at risk? Politics and governance under the ANC. *The Annals of the American Academy of Political and Social Science*, 652: 51.

respond to the challenges confronting the nation. As noted, the main challenge is that these enterprises are an unbearable burden on the national fiscus, jeopardising any economic recovery plan before it even begins.

Ramaphosa, ever the pragmatist, has focused his attention on what he regards as doable, namely, wresting the entities away from corrupt cliques that have infiltrated the institutions at both board and management levels. Ramaphosa has been able to remove a significant number of board members at Eskom, SAA, Transnet and Denel. The work was carried out through Ramaphosa's preferred strategy (discussed in Chapter 2) of setting up independent inquiries instead of getting involved in a direct confrontation by dismissing members out of hand. All Ramaphosa could be accused of is implementing recommendations by a review panel. For a president who has to walk on eggshells due to conflicting factional interests in the party, implementing recommendations by a panel makes Ramaphosa appear less vindictive than would be the case had he outright recommended the dismissal from office of individuals aligned to his political detractors.

Ramaphosa appointed his political ally Pravin Gordhan to lead the Department of Public Enterprises, with the ultimate responsibility for overseeing the clean-up of the SOEs. Ramaphosa's decision to place the SOEs under Gordhan – who emerged as a voice of reason against Zuma and his state capture project – was a strong message that the rot at the SOEs would come to an end and that the 'new dawn' had arrived. However, Gordhan's mandate at the SOEs was clear only as far as it concerned the clamping down on corruption and cleaning out of the management and board ranks.

Regarding the question of how to reorganise the SOEs and open meaningful opportunities for investment by the private sector, the minister has no mandate. It was expected that Gordhan would favour selling stakes in the SOEs to private investors in an attempt to raise funds needed to keep them operational, but politically it is much more complicated than that. The ANC has always been divided on the issue of privatisation and Cabinet's decision to partially privatise SAA could not have been an easy one.

It is difficult to imagine that Gordhan, with his pedigree in the South African Communist Party, would enthusiastically volunteer to privatise a state-owned airline. In line with his political world view, Gordhan does not favour selling the state's assets at a reduced price to private companies. Speaking to Bloomberg News in 2020 about his seeming reluctance to let go of the airline at the time,[34] I stated that I did not understand why his government was even mulling the idea of building a new state airline while it fails to stabilise an existing one. Amid lack of clarity about whether SAA would continue to exist or be done away with, Gordhan stated that 'the old SAA is dead, there is no doubt about that . . . But what will take its place may be some or all of the old SAA and maybe some other airlines too.'[35]

This is yet another indication of lack of clarity regarding the future of SAA as far as government is concerned. There seems to be a view that a properly constituted airline controlled by government with private sector investment is feasible – an idea that refuses to die among alliance partners, including Cosatu and the SACP. Within the tripartite alliance, Cosatu and the SACP have questioned the moral basis of laying off workers when unemployment is already sky-high.

---

34 Sguazzin, A. & Prinsloo, L. 2020. Gordhan stakes his reputation and South Africa's on airline. Bloomberg News, 17 May 2020. https://www.bloomberg.com/news/articles/2020-05-17/gordhan-stakes-his-reputation-and-south-africa-s-on-airline. Last accessed 14/05/2020.

35 Bloomberg. 2020. Government wants to create a new airline to take over from SAA. BusinessTech, 2 May 2020. https://businesstech.co.za/news/government/394614/government-wants-to-create-a-new-national-airline-to-takeover-from-saa/. Last accessed 14/05/2020.

The COVID-19 pandemic only increased the pressure on SAA. Even some airlines that were run successfully (for example, the Comair-operated Kulula) were facing closure due to the steep fall in traffic. Attempting to build a new airline in a hostile economic environment seems like a fool's errand, especially considering the government's track record with SAA.

If even the COVID-19 catastrophe, which brought the aviation industry to a standstill in 2020 amid restrictions on movement and the closing of borders across the world, could not shake the ANC's belief in at least partial state control of SAA, it does not bode well for future reforms. Plans to resuscitate SAA through business recue are doomed to failure under such circumstances. The strongest lobbyists against major restructuring or complete liquidation of SAA are the trade unions. Given Ramaphosa's cautious nature, it is politically difficult for him to go against both the unions and important figures in the ANC by selling a significant stake in SAA to private investors, yet the sale of 51 per cent to a strategic equity partner seems to be going ahead.

So what will become of SAA? Government's plan is that SAA will soon be owned through a partnership between it and a black-owned consortium, known as Takatso, which will own a majority share of the company. According to Gordhan, government will have a so-called non-dilutable 'golden share' of 33 per cent.

At the time of the initial announcement, the agreement was that Takatso would put in an initial R3 billion. Gordhan said that government would not be putting more money into the 'new airline' and that the name SAA would be retained.

In the end, it seems that the economic laws of gravity have prevailed over policy indecisiveness. It has become increasingly impossible for government to fund the airline, and the cash problem would have led to SAA's eventual collapse. In the 2020/2021 budget, SAA was allocated R10,5 billion while the airline remained on its deathbed under the watch of business rescue practitioners. The general public has also started to raise concerns about the SAA bailouts, given the country's other pressing needs, which included the procurement of vaccines in the fight against the COVID-19 pandemic. Yet government stood its ground and pressed for a financial bailout for SAA.

Finance minister Tito Mboweni was not keen on bailing SAA out in the latest round. Mboweni, who favours a much more market-orientated ideology than Gordhan, has openly questioned whether South Africa needs SAA.[36]

This has sparked inevitable conflict between the two ministers, with Mboweni insisting SAA is a bottomless pit and Gordhan not wanting to countenance a world without a state-owned South African airline. This has become a typical feature of Ramaphosa's Cabinet: multiple competing agendas in a seemingly unguided transition from the Zuma years.

The Eskom story is shaping up slightly differently, although it also reveals the policy schism at the heart of the ANC. Like SAA, Eskom is overseen by Gordhan's Department of Public Enterprises. However, Eskom is also a major player in government's energy strategy. Therefore, any plan to reorganise the power utility also involves the Department of Mineral Resources and Energy. This has created a policy conflict between Gordhan and the Department of Mineral Resources and Energy, which falls under ANC veteran and party chairperson Gwede Mantashe.

Mantashe has criticised the idea that Eskom is overseen by Public Enterprises while its role in the economy as an energy company is

---

36 Bloomberg. 2020. Mboweni: Do we really need SAA? BusinessTech, 23 November 2020. https://businesstech.co.za/news/government/450865/mboweni-do-we-really-need-saa/. Last accessed 14/05/2021.

dealt with by Mineral Resources and Energy. According to Mantashe, 'Eskom is an energy entity which is in DPE [the Department of Public Enterprises], not under Energy and that complicates the management of Eskom matters as some of the matters sit with DPE for approval.'[37]

When Cabinet ministers differ fundamentally about the government's organisational structure (for example, placing Eskom under the Department of Public Enterprises), it is exceedingly difficult to work towards common goals. The tensions between Gordhan and Mantashe about how to stabilise the struggling Eskom show up the lack of an overarching SOE strategy in both government and the ANC.

Both Gordhan and Mantashe are key allies of Ramaphosa, having abandoned the Zuma ship and joined the 'new dawn'. Gordhan brings a deep experience in the financial sector after his two stints as Minister of Finance. He is widely respected for his sound approach to financial management at the National Treasury and lends credibility with the private sector to Ramaphosa's Cabinet.

Mantashe, on the other hand, is a much-needed political ally in Ramaphosa's corner. He has a deep knowledge of the party's inner workings, having served two terms as secretary-general during Zuma's tenure as ANC leader. A once-staunch Zuma ally who oversaw the quelling of a revolt by some of the party branches against Zuma's leadership, Mantashe has since flipped, and he appears committed to constructing a post-Zuma dispensation. He has extensive experience in trade unions, particularly in the mining sector. Placing

---

37 Ndenze, B. 2020. Mantashe: Eskom being under DPE complicates its management. Eyewitness News, 3 February 2020. https://ewn.co.za/2020/02/21/mantashe-eskom-being-under-dpe-complicates-its-management. Last accessed 14/05/2021.

Mantashe in charge of the Mineral Resources and Energy portfolio made sense. But this is also proving to be a challenge for Ramaphosa. Appointing a minister with deeply vested interests to a portfolio at the centre of those interests can bring tensions in policy implementation, particularly in a compromise Cabinet made up of ministers with conflicting interests.

Ramaphosa's plan for Eskom is to unbundle the enterprise and allow private power producers to sell power into the national grid. Guidance and regulations regarding the implementation of this policy lie with Mantashe's department. The minister took his time before he eventually gazetted regulations about how independent power producers would be brought into the energy mix. He signed the regulations in September 2020, following criticism from business that he was stymying the policy because of his long-standing alliance with the mining trade unions, which do not favour the government's shift to renewables. As it stands, South Africa's energy sector is reliant on coal production. Any sudden shift away from coal towards renewable energy could hurt the mining industry and the unions fear mass retrenchments.

In delaying signing the regulations allowing independent power producers to feed power into the system, Mantashe appeared to have been doing the bidding of his union allies. In January 2020, Bloomberg News ran a story with the headline 'Key Ramaphosa Ally Hinders Efforts to Fix Power Supply Crisis'.[38] Mantashe took strong issue with this portrayal. The minister felt that he was being unfairly targeted by the media and business for being careful in

---

38 Burkhardt, P. & Sguazzin, A. 2020. Key Ramaphosa ally hinders efforts to fix power crisis. Bloomberg News, 20 January 2020. https://www.bloomberg.com/news/articles/2020-01-08/key-ramaphosa-ally-hinders-efforts-to-tackle-power-supply-crisis. Last accessed 14/05/2021.

carrying out a complex policy. When I was asked for an opinion by Bloomberg regarding the delays from Mantashe's office, I told the journalist that Mantashe did not believe in privatisation, so he did not like the idea of bringing private power producers into the energy mix through Eskom. After sustained criticism from business regarding how his indifference towards independent power producers was prolonging the energy crisis, Mantashe finally signed the regulations in September 2020.

The whole episode was emblematic of the ANC's muddled approach to SOEs. It is clear that the country's SOEs are at a critical stage and need to undergo urgent reforms. But the ANC is loath to implement any policy that would entail changing control and ownership of the enterprises. This allows lobby groups such as unions to influence the direction, at times pushing back against reforms that would harm their immediate interests.

Ramaphosa's Cabinet is riven by multiple agendas, contributing to the lack of direction with SOEs. This is taking place amid efforts to return the entities to sound governance and financial stability.

The reality of the power crisis at Eskom, with its economically ruinous load shedding, will likely ensure that sanity prevails and that the company is ultimately reformed. Unlike other services, whose consumption can be discretionary, electricity is an essential service and the failure of Eskom in this regard is immediate and apparent. Government cannot spin a power cut: one either has electricity or does not have it. The political and economic backlash due to power cuts have backed the ANC into a corner. Even if it is a reluctant reformer, it has little choice with regards to Eskom.

As for entities whose services are not as critical as Eskom's, the policy standoff will likely drag out in the medium term until such time that they die a natural death. This fate nearly befell SAA when the COVID-19 pandemic broke out, until government stepped in and insisted on giving the airline yet another lifeline. When SAA failed to pay salaries in May 2020,[39] speculation was that government would cut its losses and let the airline collapse. Even though this did not materialise, it was nevertheless a strong indication that at some point even the ANC government's patience could run out. It was the first time that a fiscal problem triggered panic among employees – a warning that their future at the airline is not guaranteed.

Even if Ramaphosa lacks a mandate to reform SOEs to restore their financial sustainability, he still has leverage by delaying the flow of government bailouts, gradually sending a message that the situation is untenable in the long term.

There are, of course, limitations to this strategy of firing the odd warning shot. While it sends a message regarding the long-term prospects for reforms in the system, it ignores the reality that by the time reforms are undertaken, they might be meaningless and ineffective as value would have been lost. However, this is the reality of the transformation path currently possible given the political configuration within the ANC. Outside the ANC, unions are coalescing against the privatisation of SOEs such as SAA and Eskom because of fear of job losses. The EFF, which often aligns with leftist unions, has criticised any attempt to privatise SOEs.

While the future of the SOEs is uncertain, one cannot ignore economic realities forever. Change is coming, one way or another. The ANC and the country have a clear choice about the nature of this change: reform either through a structured and orderly plan, or through a chaotic scramble when the weight of reality finally brings the roof crashing down.

---

39 Merten, M. 2020. SAA: No salaries from 1 May, R15,8bn losses over three years & still no final business rescue plan. *Daily Maverick*, 15 May 2020. https://www.dailymaverick.co.za/article/2020-05-15-saa-no-salaries-from-1-may-r15-8-billion-losses-over-three-years-still-no-final-business-rescue-plan/. Last accessed 14/05/2021.

FIVE

Paralysed by an economic war

In a divided government, President Cyril Ramaphosa has one trusted ally in his bid to push through his agenda for economic reform: the National Treasury.

This department, under the leadership of Tito Mboweni as Minister of Finance, is the one most closely aligned with Ramaphosa's thinking on the need for economic changes. This may have something to do with the reality that Treasury is sitting closer to the smouldering fire than other departments, even in the economic cluster, and can see the necessity of an urgent fiscal overhaul more clearly.

An incident in August 2019 was particularly telling with regards to where Treasury and Mboweni fit into the government's power structure. A Treasury plan for economic growth was released to the public and the media before it could be discussed within the ANC or in the tripartite alliance. The plan pushed free-market reforms to stimulate much-needed economic growth. It caused consternation among the ANC's left-wing partners, especially Cosatu and the SACP, as well as certain elements within the party itself. They were livid about the substance of the plan and about not being consulted during the process. Some of the proposals in the controversial plan included cutting red tape for new businesses and the selling of power stations.

The episode is indicative of the space that exists for Ramaphosa when it comes to economic reforms. He is mostly supported by Treasury amid the ANC's mixed economic reform messages.

My experience of engaging with players in the financial sector (namely, banking and insurance) is that Ramaphosa's presidency is focused on two core aims: the fight against corruption and a plan finally to place the economy on an upward growth trajectory. These are the twin pillars upon which the 'new dawn' rests. When Ramaphosa took over as the president of the country in 2019, unemployment was sitting at 28,8 per cent, according to Statistics South Africa.[40] High levels of unemployment result in increasing social tensions within the society, with crime on the rise. Instances of xenophobic violence are becoming more frequent, often triggered and motivated by economic destitution among young people. Statistics South Africa also showed that in 2020, 55 per cent of the youth were unemployed. This further indicates a dire situation in which half of the potentially productive portion of the population is not gainfully employed.

South Africa's GDP growth in the past decade has hardly breached the 2 per cent mark. It has become common in the past four years for the World Bank to revise South Africa's growth projection down, despite exuberance by the Reserve Bank and Treasury, often overstating growth potential. When it comes to the economy, the fundamentals are not in place and policy direction from the ruling ANC is as clear as mud. With lower levels of growth, South Africa's public sector wage bill has been growing, far outpacing salary increases in the private sector. This leaves little to be spent on much-needed infrastructure investment, a catalyst of job creation in a depressed economy. Growth in the economy will not be triggered by transfer

---

40 Statista. 2021. South Africa: Unemployment rate from 1999 to 2020. https://www.statista.com/statistics/370516/unemployment-rate-in-south-africa/. Last accessed 14/05/2021.

of salaries in the public sector. Ironically, as the public sector wage bill was ballooning during the Zuma years, capacity in the public service was declining as the tentacles of corruption stretched ever deeper into government structures.

As the ruling party, the ANC knew all this, and is to a large extent to blame for it. Now the party's discussion documents decry the 'triple challenges' of poverty, inequality and unemployment. That is the perfect storm besetting our economy. When the ANC went to its Nasrec conference that would elect Ramaphosa in December 2017, unemployment was already high (over 24 per cent) and the party was expected to attend to the ailing economy and the rising unemployment affecting the youth. During his campaign to lead the ANC, Ramaphosa promised that he would tackle the economy head-on and come up with a plan to create jobs. The ANC, however, did not take the question of the economy seriously at the conference, coming out with a concoction of policy proposals dubbed 'radical economic transformation' (RET), sparking factional conflict in the party about what ought to be the party's key intervention strategy in addressing the economy. Some in the ANC see expropriation of land without compensation as critical, while others believe that reforms in the public service and budget rationalisation are the right medicine for growth. The idea of expropriation of land without compensation and the nationalisation of the Reserve Bank are two signals from the Nasrec conference that the ANC is not interested in deep-seated economic reform, but prefers to flex its political muscles in the economic space, irrespective of the detrimental consequences for the country's fiscus.

Supporters of radical economic transformation are quick to accuse the reformers of being stooges of so-called white monopoly capital. However, the extent to which the radical economic transformation champions are embroiled in corruption and state capture has also raised suspicions that their policy positions have more to do with a vendetta against those who closed the tap of government largesse, which had flowed freely during the Zuma years. The economic policy dialogue in the ANC is in many respects a proxy war for factions in the party. This battle has led to a stalemate in terms of plans to stimulate an economy that has been battered by the COVID-19 pandemic. Besides shutting down large parts of the economy, the pandemic also overextended the state in terms of its social intervention expenditure. It is worth noting, however, that in the period leading up to the global COVID-19 outbreak, South Africa's sovereign debt was already spooking investors, and the lack of political will to address the problem was worrying sovereign rating agencies such as Moody's, Fitch and S&P, which downgraded the country's investment rating.

In the past few years, I have been able to have several conversations with rating agencies as they review South Africa periodically. One of the issues that always comes out in the discussion is the willingness of policy makers to make difficult decisions and place South Africa on a growth trajectory. The story is not as simple as I present it to be, but economic growth is going to be difficult to achieve if we continue spending the bigger part of our budget on consumption (including salaries) while leaving a paltry amount to infrastructure. No one would argue with the reality that our economy is largely growing in line with consumption, which points to debt at a household level. The sovereign rating agencies often latch on to political alignment as one of the major risks in terms of policy predictability. Investors need a sense of predictability of the system to invest for the long term. Is our politics the source of unpredictability in terms of our economic future?

Policy stability and predictability are possible when the system follows some form of underlying logic through which one can determine how decisions will be made in the future. This requires strengthening institutions over people. This is not the case with the ANC under Ramaphosa; individuals trump the ANC, because the party has been institutionally weakened by factions. This contributes to the sense that Ramaphosa and his party are on diverging economic paths. The president is aware that he has to persuade the ANC regarding reforms that are in line with budget rationalisation and the limiting of the public sector wage bill so that it does not grow further to the detriment of the fiscus. This leads us to the president's most potent outline of what he had in mind in terms of reforms: the incident in August 2019 referenced at the beginning of this chapter.

The document released by Treasury – prematurely, according to its critics – was titled 'Economic transformation, inclusive growth, and competitiveness: Towards an Economic Strategy for South Africa'.[41] It took the form of a 77-page discussion document, with specifical proposals regarding what South Africa's reforms ought to look like. In its opening, the document was quite frank regarding the state of the economy: 'The combination of low growth and rising unemployment means that South Africa's economic trajectory is unsustainable. Government should implement a series of growth reforms that promote economic transformation, support labour-intensive growth, and create a globally competitive economy.' It is a good diagnosis of South Africa's economic ills, and a sentiment widely shared in the business sector across South Africa.

In the mix of ANC internal politics, the business community has openly backed Ramaphosa and urged him to reform the economy by gaining control of the debt trajectory, among other things. Ramaphosa enjoys a reputation as someone who has a rapport with the business community, being a billionaire businessman himself with an empire ranging from mining to exotic game breeding. The re-

---

41 National Treasury, South Africa. www.treasury.gov.za.

forms proposed by Treasury were not pointing Ramaphosa in an unfamiliar direction.

Also raised in the well-articulated and comprehensive document is the challenge of concentration of ownership in the economy, with the government being urged to consider removing red tape to allow for new entrants. This is a historical problem with South Africa's economic structure: a highly concentrated economy dominated by a few conglomerates enjoying policy concessions from government, a structure that has been left untouched in the post-apartheid era. There is vast literature focusing on how the negotiations for transition in South Africa entailed not fiddling with the structure of the economy. The industrial policy approach in a democratic South Africa thus far has been dominated by big firms and organised labour, to the exclusion of small and medium businesses.[42] It therefore makes sense that this relationship would pose a challenge to new entrants to the economy, particularly for small and medium enterprises.

Treasury proposed the need to '[modernise] network industries to promote competitiveness and inclusive growth'. In this regard, efforts should be directed towards ensuring deregulation of sectors such as electricity generation to allow for independent companies to play a role. The document also proposed that the government should release additional spectrum to allow for competition in telecommunication, a catalyst to growth. The government faced criticisms about the delays in releasing the spectrum to allow competitiveness and unlock value in the digital economy.[43]

---

42 Hirsch, A. 2020. Fatal embrace: How relations between business and government help to explain South Africa's low growth equilibrium. *South African Journal of International Affairs*, 27(4): 473–492.

43 Gavasa, M. 2020. Icasa delays spectrum auction to March 2021. *TimesLIVE*, 4 September 2020. https://www.timeslive.co.za/sunday-times/business/2020-09-04-icasa-delays-spectrum-auction-to-march-2021/. Last accessed 14/05/2021.

Reduction of the 'regulatory burden' on business and the adoption of a 'flexible industrial policy' were also identified as key changes that could set South Africa on a growth path. The National Development Plan (NDP) also pointed out that a flexible industrial policy and flexible labour market were important to attract more investment and growth. Regarding the controversy surrounding land reform, it was proposed that land reform should not be only about land transfer but also about creating opportunities for more involvement of people in the sector. The document identifies the agriculture sector as one of the key areas that should be targeted for high growth and high employment since the sector is labour-intensive. This is one of the issues that I have pressed for a long time: that South Africa should optimise the agriculture sector in creating jobs and addressing the spatial challenges. The ANC's plan for agriculture, however, seems to be different from what is proposed by Treasury. As such, the Treasury document was a timely warning to the ANC about its politics-focused land reform, when it should instead be paying attention to economic imperatives.

A few weeks after Treasury's proposal was released, Reuters news agency ran a story with the headline 'Business leaders urge South Africa's Ramaphosa to reform faster'.[44] Interestingly, the document stated that business in South Africa is surviving in an environment of policy uncertainty. Business publications wrote editorials urging the government to take the high road and begin implementing reforms. Of course, the ANC is responsible for this standstill since the party is unable to show policy coherence. The document emphasises macroeconomic stability and fiscal stability as key. A closer

---

44 Reuters. 2019. Business leaders urge South Africa's Ramaphosa to reform faster. 4 September 2019. https://www.reuters.com/article/us-wef-africa-ramaphosa/business-leaders-urge-south-africas-ramaphosa-to-reform-faster-idINKCN1VP0W8. Last accessed 14/05/21.

look at the gist of what was proposed by Treasury points to the ANC as the weakest link in South Africa's policy machinery. There are complex reasons why the ANC will not readily support what Treasury proposed.

The proposals would require the ANC-led government to change its attitude towards SOEs, including Eskom. By allowing private companies to play a role in sectors that have been traditionally the exclusive purview of government policy, Treasury's proposal would displace the ANC. The delays in releasing the spectrum in the telecommunications sector also have to do with the influence of special interests. Some of the distortions identified by Treasury in South Africa's policy framework are created by the ANC; particularly in instances where reforms would loosen the party's political hold over society. For example, the ANC is finding it difficult to imagine how it will influence policy without controlling levers such as Eskom or SAA. The party struggles to formulate a transformation agenda that does not involve controlling procurement at SOEs.

As noted, the proposal by Treasury was met with criticism from Cosatu and the SACP. Alliance partners criticised Mboweni for releasing the document to the public before it had been discussed internally within the alliance. Some within the ANC were also not interested in elevating the document to a higher standing, while allies of Ramaphosa supported the reform proposals. When I was asked why Treasury had released the document to the public before it had been processed within the party or in the alliance, I pointed out that it had been done deliberately so that it could reach the public before the alliance tore it apart. Through a trusted ally at Treasury, Ramaphosa realised it was better for the broader public or stakeholders outside the ANC and the alliance to formulate their view on the proposals before the alliance partners and some within the ANC could kill it. The document enjoys strong support in the business sector; however, it has received mixed reactions within the ANC and the alliance.

The possibility of a sovereign downgrade did not instil an urgency in the ANC, nor did it show a shift towards the type of reforms outlined by Ramaphosa through Treasury. Ramaphosa's detractors in the ANC were even more driven to push for implementation of the ANC's Nasrec resolutions, including the nationalisation of the Reserve Bank – sending a strong signal that the party is not about to embrace the market-friendly reforms that essentially require it to relinquish some key areas of policy influence, including control of SOEs. In the last quarter of 2019, since Treasury's proposal was released, the ANC-led government has not made any move showing that Treasury's proposals were to be implemented. Treasury would remain an isolated department in the government, standing against the bailout of SAA in the 2021 budget. SAA was finally allocated a bailout to the tune of R10,5 billion. A defeated Mboweni then got on with the mopping-up work, stating that the allocation 'was not a bailout, but a funding to help SAA through business rescue'. Whatever Mboweni prefers to call it, the money came from reprioritisation from other programmes that are more important than maintaining SAA under its current circumstances.

If the imminent possibility of sovereign downgrading and sheer economic destitution was not sufficient to get the ANC to panic and consider implementing some of the reforms, then one would think that the outbreak of a global pandemic would achieve such results. But the policy standstill that prevailed regarding reforms has persisted, even after COVID-19 brought South Africa's economy to its knees. In the early weeks of the outbreak in 2020, I watched closely to see whether Ramaphosa would be able to use the crisis moment and implement some of the economic reforms. My view was that the temporary freezing of politics under the lockdown and the support the president was enjoying as a commander-in-chief leading a nation in crisis would give Ramaphosa the political capital he needed to expedite key decisions that under normal circumstances would face political resistance.

At the start of the COVID-19 pandemic, in March 2020, South Africa was further downgraded by the rating agency Moody's to Ba1, otherwise known as full junk status.[45] It all pointed to an unsustainable debt trajectory and the lack of political will to manage the growing public sector wage bill. I discussed some of those issues with rating agencies as they carried out their review of the country during the pandemic. The feeling was that infighting within the ANC was keeping the party from attending to important challenges such as the economy. The appetite for reforms in the ANC was still lacking. In November 2020, Moody's further downgraded South Africa to Ba2, pushing the country two levels below investment grade. That is not a direction in which to be headed with an economy growing at less than 1 per cent and the losses caused by the pandemic yet to be fully comprehended.

In August 2020, in the middle of the pandemic and with an economic contraction not seen in recent times, Parliament began discussion about a Bill on nationalisation of the Reserve Bank, one of the resolutions of the ANC adopted at the 2017 Nasrec conference. The bill was popular among Ramaphosa's detractors, who saw it as a victory against the president's private-sector allies. The decision to move ahead with the Bill signalled that the ANC was not heeding the effect of the pandemic on the economy as the party pushed on with its radical economic transformation agenda.

---

45 Bloomberg. 2020. South Africa to full junk status. BusinessTech, 28 March 2020. https://businesstech.co.za/news/finance/385575/south-africa-downgraded-to-full-junk-status/. Last accessed 14/05/2021.

Instead of shifting in the direction of embracing reforms, or some elements thereof, the ANC seems to be reading the impact of COVID-19 in a different way, leading the party in the opposite direction. According to the ANC, the experience of the COVID-19 pandemic has made it necessary to create a state-owned pharmaceutical company. The ANC came out of one of its NEC meetings in December 2020 with a resolve to establish such a company.[46] This throws the logic of reforms into a moral crisis. According to many party members and allies, the job losses incurred during the pandemic render job cuts in SOEs morally indefensible. For example, the effect of the pandemic on job losses was one of the arguments made against the decision by the SABC management to retrench what they call 'redundant workers' at the national broadcaster. The pandemic will most likely be used by policy hardliners to justify more state intervention and a stronger regulatory hand in the system. The challenges confronted in the health sector during the pandemic also threw the spotlight on the drive to implement the controversial National Health Insurance (NHI) programme, which aims to centralise health provision under government control.

It is not an entirely South African phenomenon that the COVID-19 pandemic would encourage policy overreach by government. In the case of South Africa, however, the government is confronted with a perennial capacity challenge, including the problem of corruption, which often scavenges on public policy. Whenever the government is extending its involvement in a sector or in people's lives, questions emerge about the affordability of such a step and whether there is capacity to implement the idea. The reading by

---

46 SABC. 2020. ANC calls for establishment of state-owned pharmaceutical company. 10 December 2020. https://www.sabcnews.com/sabcnews/anc-calls-for-an-establishment-of-a-state-owned-pharmaceutical-company/. Last accessed 14/05/2021.

some within the ANC (namely, the radical economic transformation camp) is that the government should become more involved in delivery of public goods instead of focusing on encouraging competitiveness in the provision of goods and services. For them, the involvement of the government will lead to competitiveness. Past experience – at Eskom, for example – does not bode well for this approach.

Ramaphosa's decision to approach the International Monetary Fund (IMF) for a US$4,3 billion loan to manage the immediate consequences of the pandemic also highlighted the faultlines in the ANC. In the process of negotiating the loan, the IMF established certain conditions, such as the need for South Africa to adopt reforms and rebuild its economy. The IMF would have a problem with its funding being used to pay public sector salaries. Senior ANC members raised their concerns about accepting a World Bank loan with conditions attached that could affect South Africa's sovereignty. Finance Minister Mboweni assured his comrades in the ANC that the loans would not allow the IMF to dictate to South Africa. However, what will ultimately dictate to South Africa is the reality that at some point things will just not be able to carry on this way. The question is how and when that moment will arise.

The policy standoff among ANC members at Nasrec can only be resolved at the party's next elective conference to see who prevails between Ramaphosa and his detractors in the party. If Ramaphosa wins the next presidency of the ANC, he will have attained the mandate he needs to implement reforms. The opposite also applies: if he loses, his project will have been rejected. While this situation persists, some reforms need to be implemented. One thing that sets Ramaphosa apart from his predecessors is that he has allowed governance failures in some departments to escalate to an operational crisis. There are more such cases emerging across the public service where rationalisation is imposed by immediate circumstances.

Despite differences in the ANC and a lack of direction, failure to pay salaries is an experience as real as the force of gravity and will certainly compel reforms. When they become inevitable, reforms will be implemented.

The problem with this path is that it is a disjointed and haphazard approach. One day the president is telling people that radical economic transformation will be implemented, and the next SAA further deteriorates so that it becomes inevitable to liquidate the airline once and for all. This does not look like a coherent strategy, but this is what is on offer in the current political configuration in the country.

When it comes to the economy, Ramaphosa has been in search of the elusive consensus to get key stakeholders to pull in the same direction. Labour, business and political leaders have not been talking the same language. According to the business sector, political leaders have not been helpful in using policy instruments to unlock value in our economy; they have been pursuing sectarian interests at the expense of all, the argument goes. According to political leaders, business has not been honest and forthcoming in investing in the country's economy. They have been talking down the country's stock, and taking away massive profits not matched by their levels of investment in the economy. Completing the troika is labour, which believes that workers' interests are always trampled upon by business in its unholy alliance with the political elites. Meanwhile, business believes that labour is holding government, and everyone, to ransom by extorting protection through rigid labour laws.

In response to this, Ramaphosa proposed a 'social compact' to bring key stakeholders together to tread a way forward based on national interest. Ramaphosa may not yet see the success of his efforts to place the country on a different trajectory after the disastrous Zuma years, during which the economy was the least of Zuma's priorities, but Ramaphosa has at least paved the way for the reflection the country needs. The ideological maze of reforms will be cleared as economic reality sets in. This will eventually precipitate changes, but in the meantime, every day of ANC policy paralysis weakens our economy a little bit more.

SIX
A breach in the giant's defences

At national and provincial level, South Africa's politics can sometimes look like a stagnant pool of water, whose levels rise and fall slightly according to the rainfall. On the local level, it is closer to a free-flowing river, with some rapids along the way.

For nearly three decades, the ANC's support in national elections has not moved beyond the band of 57,5 per cent (in 2019) and 69,69 per cent (in 2004). On the provincial level, only one province, the Western Cape, has ever fallen into the hands of the opposition.

Locally, the picture looks a lot different. Besides controlling a host of smaller municipalities, especially in the Western Cape, and the medium-sized Midvaal council in the Vaal Triangle, the opposition has at various times ruled in four of South Africa's major metro regions: Johannesburg, Tshwane, Cape Town and Nelson Mandela Bay. Of course, this has much to do with urban areas being a more favourable hunting ground for the opposition parties than the rural areas.

However, the local government system is also inherently more dynamic than our national and provincial systems. This is thanks to a mixed electoral system that allows residents to vote directly for a particular candidate to represent their ward, in addition to a system of proportional representation that allocates a specific number of councillors to each qualifying party based on the number of votes it receives. The inclusion of direct representation in the local government system deepens democracy and accountability at this level, according to its proponents.

In local or municipal elections, each voter receives two ballots. On one ballot, the voter chooses between political parties to represent him or her in the council, and on the other, for the candidate who will represent his or her area in the same council. In some small local municipalities, voters get an additional third ballot to vote for a party to represent them in a district council on a proportional basis.

The local government system opens the door for independent candidates to contest seats without the muscle of a formal political party behind them.

Champions of electoral reform in South Africa argue that the local government system offers a blueprint for national and provincial elections. They contend that a constituency-based electoral system, where members of Parliament or provincial legislatures are elected directly by voters, would increase accountability. These representatives, so the argument goes, would be more likely to remain loyal to their constituents than to their party.

The failure of ANC MPs to hold the executive branch accountable during the state capture years – preferring to march in lockstep with the Zuma faction – is grist to the mill of these arguments. The ANC MPs' loyalty was first and foremost to the party that had selected them for the ANC's proportional list.

The push for greater direct representation in Parliament has received the backing of no a less a figure than Deputy Chief Justice Raymond Zondo. During one of the hearings of the Zondo Commission, Zondo remarked that a constituency system may be one way to increase accountability.

Overall, it looks as if proponents of more direct representation are gaining ground. Aaron Motsoaledi, Minister of Home Affairs, has told Parliament that electoral reform is necessary. A report commissioned by the Inclusive Society Institute has recommended greater direct representation, following in the footsteps of the late Frederik van Zyl Slabbert, whose task team famously recommended in 2002 that a constituency-based system combined with proportional representation was the way forward. The Inclusive Society Institute's team was led by Roelf Meyer, the National Party government's chief negotiator at Codesa, and included Professor William Gumede, political analyst Ebrahim Fakir and Dren Nupen, former executive director of the Electoral Institute of Southern Africa. It recommended that 300 of the 400 seats in the National Assembly be allocated on the basis of a constituency-based system and the remaining 100 by a proportional system.

A Constitutional Court judgment in June 2020 about the rights of independent candidates to stand in national and provincial elections (the *New Nation* judgment) could also be a catalyst for change.[47] The court found that the Electoral Act of 1998 is unconstitutional 'to the extent that it requires that adult citizens may be elected to the National Assembly and Provincial Legislatures only through their membership of political parties'.

With this judgment, the court introduced into the national and provincial spheres of government a feature that has thus far only been a character of our local government system. It sets South Africa on an unpredictable electoral reform path that would require a complex redesign, including a formula through which seats in the provincial and national legislatures must be allocated among proportional and constituency representatives.

---

47 *New Nation Movement NPC and Others v President of the Republic of South Africa and* Others (CCT110/19) [2020] ZACC 11; 2020 (8) BCLR 950 (CC); 2020 (6) SA 257 (CC) (11 June 2020).

It is apparent in the *New Nation* judgment that the court views an arrangement involving direct representation as institutionally superior to one relying on proportional representation alone. When it comes to laws, regulations and other instruments, local government in South Africa has it all in place. Since the first democratic municipal elections were held in 1996, a raft of legislation has been implemented, aimed at strengthening the local government sphere.

Yet, for all the theoretical advantages of our local government system, they have – for the most part – not paid off in practice. Service delivery has collapsed completely in some rural towns, while many more have municipalities in dire financial distress.

The release of the Auditor-General's report on municipal finances has become an annual horror show, as predictable as the release of a new *Friday the 13th* horror movie once was.

In July 2020, the then Auditor-General Kimi Makwetu once again painted a picture of municipalities where financial mismanagement has become a rule, with good management being the exception. In the municipal audit results report for 2018/19 issued in 2020, Makwetu summed up the twin problems bedevilling our municipalities as follows: 'Not much to go around, yet not the right hands at the till.'

Irregular expenditure keeps rising, as rampant corruption and nepotism siphons off the money meant to deliver services to ratepayers.

Some of the stories emerging from our municipalities are scarcely believable, such as Tlhalefi Mashamaite, the mayor of the Mogalakwena Municipality in Limpopo, amassing 27 bodyguards during a factional battle with members of his own party as well as the municipal manager.[48] Before finally being fired, Mashamaite had

---

48 News24. 2015. ANC finally gives mayor with 27 bodyguards the boot. 2 July 2015. https://www.news24.com/News24/ANC-finally-gives-mayor-with-27-bodyguards-the-boot-20150602. Last accessed 14/05/2021.

also gone on a spending spree that included buying 12 000 T-shirts to the tune of R838 000. The T-shirts were supposed to be handed out at so-called outreach gatherings hosted by the mayor.

One could fill a whole book with stories such as these.

In Makwetu's report, only 20 of the country's 257 municipalities received a clean audit. Of these 257 municipalities, 28 of them were not even audited because they failed to submit their financial statements. About 200 municipalities lost about R2,07 billion over the financial year, and irregular spending increased from R24,38 billion in 2017/2018 to R32,06 billion in 2018/2019.

Financial mismanagement and outright corruption are not the only hurdles faced by municipalities. One of the biggest additional problems is that many have lost touch with their residents, resulting in misplaced priorities and misdirected initiatives.

Local councillors and officials are supposed to be the labourers at the coalface of democracy. It is the form of government closest to the day-to-day lives of citizens. If it performs, they flourish. If it stumbles, they suffer.

The Constitution states that local government should 'provide democratic and accountable government for local communities; [and also] . . . ensure the provision of services to communities in a sustainable manner'.[49]

South Africa has a long history of repressive local government in the form of municipalities and homeland authorities through which communities were policed and controlled during apartheid years. I have covered this area in other work, with extensive discussion on the importance of public participation in strengthening local gov-

---

49 Constitution of the Republic of South Africa, Act 108 of 1996, Section 152 (a, b).

ernment.⁵⁰ If people's interaction with local government is positive, this leads to the strengthening of the country's democracy as a whole.

In my experience as a field researcher across South Africa's municipalities, the quality of public participation is poor and citizens generally feel they are not consulted at local government level, with a few pockets of exceptions. Since residents do not meaningfully participate in planning processes, municipalities tend to have misplaced priorities, showing that they are not in touch with the communities they are supposed to serve.

When it comes to the consolidation of our democracy and the strengthening of our democratic institutions, South Africa's local government is a monumental letdown.

For many, protests have become the preferred method of political engagement at local government level. While it is easy to bemoan the destruction of property that often accompanies these protests, one has to ask why citizens feel that this is the only effective way to make their voices heard.

While some protest, a significant part of impoverished rural populations have largely resigned themselves to living under conditions of poor service delivery and rampant looting of public resources. Basic services such as water and roads are either not delivered at all, or, if they have been delivered, the infrastructure needed to support them has been neglected to the point where their delivery is severely compromised.

Far from contributing towards the consolidation of our democracy,

---

50 Mathekga, R. & Baccus, I. 2006. The challenge of local government structures in South Africa: Securing community participation. *Critical Dialogue: Public Participation in Review*; Mathekga, R. 2006. Participatory government and the challenge of inclusion: The case of local government structures in post apartheid South Africa. *Colombia Internacional, 63*.

municipalities have become a point of crisis. Because of their central role in the lives of citizens, the continued failure of local government could spell trouble for the broader democratic project in the country.

Here and there specks of light shine through, offering a glimpse of what is possible in our local government system. In the Nelson Mandela Bay metro, a DA coalition government that lasted two years was able to stop the worst excesses of the previous administration – described in horrific detail by Crispian Olver in his book *How to Steal a City*. The ANC-run Capricorn District Municipality in Limpopo won plaudits from the Auditor-General for the improvements in its internal controls. 'Capricorn District should inspire confidence in other municipalities to prove that where internal control systems are implemented, key vacancies are filled and there is stability at management level, a clean audit outcome is within reach,' the report said.[51]

But, despite the fact that South Africa has a good local government system on paper, the story of South Africa's municipalities is still mostly a tale of woe.

Why is the institutional infrastructure that has been adopted to put local government on a strong footing not working? I believe a big reason is the long-standing ambivalence in the ANC about the establishment of a capable local government sphere that is effective and autonomous of the national sphere of government. A strong and coherent local government could result in political power drifting away from the central government, which is the ANC's first priority. Self-sufficient, capable municipalities that are able to deliver on

---

51 Business Insider SA. 2020. These are the best-run municipalities in SA – including Midvaal and Okhahlamba in KZN. 5 July 2020. https://www.businessinsider.co.za/well-run-municipalities-including-midvaal-and-and-okhahlamba-in-kzn-2020-7. Last accessed 14/05/2021.

their mandate autonomously, with little help or interference by central government, are a worthy goal but not necessarily for an organisation steeped in centralism (see Chapter 1). During South Africa's negotiations on the road to democracy in the early 1990s, the ANC did not favour a strong devolution of powers to provinces and local government.[52] It preferred a strong unitary state with the three spheres of government remaining dependent upon one another. The party was concerned that federalism would maintain some of apartheid's demarcations, such as 'homelands', making it difficult for the party to build a united South Africa based on shared values. The idea was to avoid the creation of separate power centres, which, according to the party's thinking, would make transformation of the broader society difficult. Simply put, the ANC feared that a strong federal system would dilute the political power of the ANC at the centre.

This case against strong federalism or institutionally independent municipalities was built on abstract foundations. After three decades of practical experience with local government, we can now say that the ANC's plan to keep municipalities on a leash by ensuring that they remain subservient to the national sphere of government has failed. Through its policy of cadre deployment, the ANC inspires loyalty but not competence.

It is widely accepted that the DA, for all its own problems, does a much better job than the ANC of running municipalities. Few would argue that the DA-led Cape Town metro is the best-run city government in the country.

Under the leadership of its young mayor, Bongani Baloyi, the

---

52 Powell, D. 2010. Transition to cooperative federalism: The South African experience. *Forum of Federations*, 2010, Number 3. http://www.forumfed.org/pubs/OPS3_Transition_Cooperative_Federalism_TheSouthAfrican_Experience.pdf. Last accessed 14/05/2021.

DA-run Midvaal municipality is also one of the few glimmers of light on an otherwise bleak horizon. 'The municipal culture, driven by both the political and administrative leadership, is characterised by zero tolerance for transgressions and by taking personal accountability for maintaining good financial practices and sustaining clean audit outcomes,' the Auditor-General noted.[53] The Midvaal municipality also managed to avoid one of the biggest pitfalls of governments and state institutions at all levels in South Africa: overspending on salaries and leaving too little in the kitty for developing and maintaining infrastructure. Baloyi's municipality spent only 24 per cent of its total revenue of R1,16 billion on salaries.

As noted at the beginning of this chapter, the ANC has started to pay a price at the ballot box for its struggles at the municipal level, which theoretically should spur it into action in abandoning its failed local government philosophy.

The local government elections in 2016 showed that the party had reason to be concerned. After receiving 64,8 per cent of the vote in 2006 and 61,95 per cent in 2011, the party tumbled to 53,9 per cent in 2016.[54] While the ANC's share of the vote dropped by 8 percentage points, the opposition DA managed to garner 26,9 per cent, compared to its 2011 showing of 19,59 per cent – in part a reward for its reputation for competent governance at this level. The party also gained enough votes in the Johannesburg, Tshwane and Nelson Mandela Bay metro areas to be able to form coalition city governments. The triumph in the three metros represented the first significant breach in the giant's defences outside the Western Cape.

---

53 Business Insider SA. 2020. These are the best-run municipalities in SA – including Midvaal and Okhahlamba in KZN. 5 July 2020. https://www.businessinsider.co.za/well-run-municipalities-including-midvaal-and-and-okhahlamba-in-kzn-2020-7. Last accessed 14/05/2021.
54 Electoral Commission of South Africa. www.elections.org.za.

If the DA wants to have any hope of one day slaying its foe, it needs to maintain and emphasise its record of excellence at local and provincial government level, rather than being fixated on fighting identity politics wars.

In the meantime, a big debate is looming about whether South Africa's struggling municipalities should retain all of their responsibilities and powers. It is unlikely that an ANC government would rescue municipalities by strengthening them institutionally as capable and autonomous spheres of government. Instead, the ANC favours consolidation of municipalities into bigger regions (or districts) to deal with the political fallout due to the party's decline at local government level. As the ANC is losing control of municipalities, the response has been to shift power from local to national government under the pretence of pursuing development goals that are of national importance and which cannot be left to ailing municipalities plagued by severe capacity challenges.

To deal with the crisis at local government level, the ANC government proposed the District Development Model as a move to consolidate municipalities into fewer development districts. Dubbed a 'game changer', the District Development Model 'aims to improve the coherence and impact of government service delivery with focus on 44 districts and 8 metros around the country as development spaces that can be used as centres of service delivery and economic development, including job creation'.[55] Ramaphosa has mentioned the model a few times since 2019, to emphasise a shift towards co-ordination of action at local government level. Or is it more than just coordination?

In the public policy discourse the district model has not gained

---

55 Department of Cooperative Governance and Traditional Affairs. n.d. District Development Model. https://www.cogta.gov.za/ddm/. Last accessed 14/05/2021.

much traction, simply because the challenges faced by municipalities are not related to coordination problems. Of course, government should always strive to coordinate plans across the country to ensure seamless implementation. However, the coordination approach suggested through the district model would remove planning power from municipalities, since it is the national government that would drive the process. A pilot project for the District Development Model was undertaken in 2020 under the leadership of the Department of Cooperative Governance and Traditional Affairs.

Amid a crisis at local government, it is a possible solution that looks attractive to the ANC – which, as an organisation, usually favours centralising power instead of devolving it. However, a political party in the position of the DA – which has had more success in governing municipalities – could find the district model to be an undue encroachment by national government on local government. Critics of the approach see it as a desperate effort by the ANC to use its power at the national level to gain political control of the local government sphere, which is being lost to other political parties in the electoral process. Because corruption has been rampant across municipalities under the ANC, fears are that the district model will centralise corruption instead of uprooting it.

Centralisation of power is not a long-term solution to the problems encountered in our public service. It presupposes that, somewhere out there, there are a few great people who can be trusted to make key decisions for society. In the case of the district model, there is the questionable idea that the national sphere of government has the capacity, the will and the determination always to act in the interests of all municipalities across the country.

The ANC has also been flirting with the idea of reducing the number of provinces, which would have a similar centralising effect. In policy documents, the ANC has stated that 'the ongoing assessment of the configuration of the state, in most cases, points to the need for a review of key policy and constitutional issues. Among others, these include the allocation of powers and functions, planning across government, the two-tier system of local government, and the effectiveness and functionality of some provinces.'[56] As far back as the ANC's 52nd National Conference, held in 2007, the party has never let go of the idea of reconfiguring the relationship between the three spheres of government, particularly regarding the powers and responsibilities of local and provincial governments. Again, this harks back to the ANC's long-held suspicion of strong federalism.

When it comes to the party's plans to reconfigure the provincial and local government structure, the stage seems set for a protracted conflict in the courts. There seems to be a perception within the ANC that the current configuration is there because the ANC wanted it to be and the party can simply do away with it when it pleases in its attempt to address a service delivery crisis of its own making. This belief is misguided. The current configuration is the result of a political negotiation process that has been sealed in the Constitution. Any attempt to reduce the number of provinces would have to clear some high constitutional hurdles.

The task of reviewing the nature of intergovernmental relations across the three spheres of government is not the exclusive terrain of the ANC. The District Development Model has been sold by government as a quick-fix solution, an intervention that does not need wide discussion. However, the Constitution requires public participation as an essential part of planning. If planning and execution are moved further away from the people through a policy of coordination or centralisation, a constitutional question arises.

---

56 Monama, T. 2017. Fewer provinces on the cards. IOL, 21 May 2017. https://www.iol.co.za/capetimes/news/fewer-provinces-on-the-cards-9264454. Last accessed 14/05/2021.

Potential opposition to the plans is not limited to opposition parties such as the DA. Centralisation of power in the state could also upset the political balance within the ANC, with regional leaders decrying undue interference from central leadership of the party through national departments. Widespread mismanagement at a local and provincial level will, however, make it difficult for ANC members to advance this argument when their own house is not in order.

As democratic consolidation gets underway, political leaders even within the ANC will realise the importance of a properly governed local municipality as a basis for showcasing political leadership. Not all deployed ANC members are content to let corruption and mismanagement slide. Some feel that good governance is possible if the party desists from interfering and allows local leaders to manage municipalities efficiently. Some also oppose the centralisation of power because of its impact on democratisation. The political trend in relation to local government should be a shift towards further decentralisation and ensuring accountability by leaders.

So far, there are not many examples of leaders successfully using local government to showcase political leadership, except in the case of the DA. For leaders to ascend to national politics, they should first and foremost demonstrate that they can effectively manage municipalities. Currently, this pipeline is blocked. A strong constituency system practised at national level would help to create a bridge between municipal and national government, with well-regarded local leaders having a greater chance to emerge from the ground level and enter Parliament. This could elevate local government to its rightful place and create an incentive for good governance that is attuned to the needs of local citizens.

Despite the challenges confronting local government, the sphere is evolving beyond the comprehension of some ANC leaders. The

Constitutional Court's decision that individuals should be able to be elected to the national Parliament without having to stand on a party ticket has paved the way for South Africa to embrace the constituency system. Such a change would also shake local government politics.

The ANC's plan to fiddle with the municipalities is at odds with the judgment in the *New Nation* case. Centralisation goes against the principle of the constituency system, and the ANC should reconsider its position on this.

Despite the ANC's efforts, the next decade holds much promise for local government. If strong linkages can be formed between local government and a possible constituency system, the sector will establish itself as proving ground for future leaders. Progressive evolution of local government is almost a natural phenomenon in a democracy, and it would take much effort for any party to manage or even block this trend. In my view, in the next few decades it will matter less and less who the president of the country is, but it will matter more and more who the mayor of one's town or city is. Cities are becoming stronger centres of government, and some politicians have no interest in running the country or a province but are interested in consolidating power in cities – especially cities that are economic hubs.

This is the philosophy espoused by businessman-turned-politician Herman Mashaba, who resigned as mayor of Johannesburg in October 2019 after an acrimonious split with the DA. Mashaba and I have had our differences. After I criticised him about his penchant for right-wing populism, as shown in his anti-immigration stance, he hit back in an opinion piece, arguing that it is difficult to run a political party and I am welcome to try it out.

Despite my criticism of some aspects of Mashaba's agenda, I am nonetheless impressed by the boldness of his politics. He does not feel bound by the ANC's transformation agenda and preaches a form of prosperity politics. Mashaba was not happy within the DA because of its stance on race. He accused the party of being in denial about the effect that one's skin colour has on access to opportunities. For Mashaba, who made his money as a businessman, race matters in South Africa.

Even so, Mashaba does not believe that the ANC's transformation remedy is the way to go. He has identified a niche that opposition parties do not see: to promote and implement progressive policy measures at local government level. Speaking to Mashaba after his resignation from the DA, I asked him whether he wanted to start a party that would contest elections at national level. He replied that he was more interested in gaining control of Gauteng's cities, managing them properly and expanding their economic strength.

The dynamics of the cities in Gauteng are the same and they can be mobilised as centres of power. Who cares who governs Gauteng province if that person is not in charge of the City of Tshwane, the City of Johannesburg and the City of Ekurhuleni? Regional political mobilisation is highly concentrated in those cities at local government level. As the grip of the central government weakens, local government will become a strategic area of focus, a new centre of power in an environment of multiple centres of power.

The ANC's plan to emasculate local government by turning it into a glorified service delivery desk responsible for filling potholes is destined to fail.

The party would do well to rethink its approach to this sector. Its once impregnable dam wall has already sprung some leaks in the major metros. If the ANC does not get its municipal house in order, that trickle will eventually become a flood, unleashing a torrent of water that could engulf even a giant.

SEVEN

The stumbling opposition

Ever since South Africa embarked on democracy in 1994, the ANC has dominated political processes significantly, dwarfing opposition parties that have only a paltry influence on the system. The ANC has had almost unlimited success in national and provincial elections since then and no opposition party has been able to unseat the ANC at the national level.

The DA has achieved some success on the provincial level, taking over the Western Cape province in 2009, fifteen years after the first instalment of democratic elections.

However, the picture has been changing in the past few years, with opposition politics undergoing interesting shifts. The DA and the EFF have begun challenging the ANC's moral authority to lead society, questioning the party's transformation project and its viability to take South Africa forward.

Both the DA and EFF were instrumental in Jacob Zuma's early resignation as president in February 2018. Zuma faced relentless onslaughts from them through a series of court cases, including an attempt to impeach him after the Public Protector found he had benefited improperly from upgrades to his homestead at Nkandla in rural KwaZulu-Natal. The Constitutional Court consequently decided in favour of the EFF that the National Assembly had shirked its responsibility in not holding Zuma to account. It led to unsuccessful impeachment proceedings against him. However, the opposition made Zuma's visits to Parliament so difficult that the ANC eventually conceded that he had become a liability, pushing him to resign in 2018. He practically left office to the sound of the chant: 'Pay back the money!'

It was during the Zuma years that South Africa's opposition shone and gave a glimpse of what could happen if they shared common goals. Let's face it, the DA and EFF differ a great deal. However, their common dislike of Zuma created a bond between the two parties. Had it not been for the EFF, with their insistence that they would disrupt Zuma in Parliament until he resigned, the ANC would have played dead and continued with Zuma as leader until the 2019 elections when his term in government was supposed to come to an end. That could easily have given Zuma's allies an opportunity to consolidate their hold on the state and its key institutions, and to counter the incoming Cyril Ramaphosa.

Once Zuma had been replaced by Ramaphosa, however, the two major opposition parties began experiencing internal turmoil, as they reconstituted themselves in opposition to Ramaphosa's presidency. They suddenly had to rethink their short-term strategies.

The DA views Ramaphosa as a moderate and someone with whom it can work, despite the differences it has with the ANC. It somehow sees Ramaphosa as someone held ransom by the ANC.

For the EFF, Ramaphosa represents corporate South Africa's interests.

Ironically, the EFF borrowed the Bell Pottinger term once coined to protect the interests of the Zuma camp – 'white monopoly capital' – to define Ramaphosa's relationship with certain groups. The Gupta family, who employed Bell Pottinger, wanted to infiltrate debates in South Africa to ensure that Zuma's project of radical economic transformation gained momentum so that they could cash in on government deals. The EFF took the same script and applied it to Ramaphosa, resulting in the party taking inexplicable stands on some key political issues. For example, it started supporting embattled Public Protector Busisiwe Mkhwebane, who has been accused of being a flag bearer for a specific faction in the ANC.[57]

Since Zuma left office, the EFF has been left morally exposed and it is becoming increasingly difficult to make sense of the party's position on corruption, for example.

The EFF would say it supports anti-corruption measures, but it does not support Ramaphosa's version because it does not include investigating corruption involving his allies in the private sector and the political arena – including Pravin Gordhan.

The EFF has been consumed by the Gordhan matter. It is an example of the EFF's tendency to pursue personality politics. It identifies individuals with whom it fights proxy battles to distract from problems within the party or the personal benefits that some of the EFF's leaders are experiencing.

This is one of the favourite techniques of Julius Malema, leader of the party. He was Zuma's ally before they fell out in 2012, resulting in Malema's expulsion from the ANC. I have covered, at great length, how Malema thereafter crafted an anti-Zuma political space, pursuing politics of disruption,[58] or anti-establishment politics. However, Malema learnt from Zuma during the latter's earlier troubles with the law.

The gripe between Malema and Gordhan could be traced back to an investigation by SARS into Malema's tax affairs. The revenue service initiated the only successful state action against Malema that has had personal consequences: he lost his half-built house

---

57 Steenhuisen, J. 2021. Getting rid of RET Protector Busisiwe Mkhwebane. Politicsweb, 10 March 2021. https://www.politicsweb.co.za/opinion/getting-rid-of-ret-protector-busisiwe-mkhwebane. Last accessed 14/05/2021.
58 Mathekga, R. 2018. *Ramaphosa's Turn*. Cape Town: Tafelberg.

in the posh Gauteng suburb of Sandton after it was attached to pay his debt to SARS. It was sold at auction for R5,9 million.

The government body did not lose focus after that. It eventually also obtained warrants to attach moveable property worth millions from Adriano Mazzotti, co-owner of the tobacco company Carnilinx. Malema had earlier admitted that he had received a loan from Carnilinx of R1 million and that the EFF had received a donation of R200 000 from the company.[59]

Gordhan, an administrator with huge experience in the fields of taxes and state finances, secured SARS's victory against Malema, a victory that Malema saw as a politically motivated machination. He would fight Gordan and anyone who dared stand next to him from then on.

As a political party that is supposed to target institutions and centres of power, the EFF finds itself chasing after Gordhan like wild dogs going after a wounded beast, wasting energy and resources on political fights that will not dent the capitalist system they are apparently revolting against. It is difficult to comprehend what the strategic value could be of fighting Gordhan. The party's politics is clear as mud.

However, one thing is clear: the situation is made more complex by the personal legal troubles faced by key leaders of the party.

Malema learnt from Zuma that anti-establishment politics are more effective when infused with some genuine concerns within the society. The local depth of poverty and inequality has created a captive audience for such politics.

Since the EFF was only created after Malema left the ANC, thus

---

59 *The Citizen*. 2019. Sars seizes EFF funder Mazzotti's property over R70m debt. 19 February 2019. https://citizen.co.za/news/south-africa/breaking-news/2086536/sars-seizes-eff-funder-mazzottis-property-over-r70m-debt/. Last accessed 14/05/2021.

long after the 1994 elections, the EFF feels it can disrupt the system without having to explain itself. For example, the party disrupted Zuma without society even questioning Malema's earlier role in propping Zuma up as ANC leader. Had it not been for Malema, Zuma might not have made it to the position, or become leader of the country.

Malema has volunteered a mild apology for supporting Zuma earlier, but at the same time visits him when he can benefit from such a meeting. For example, he had tea with Zuma in February 2021 following the former president's announcement that he would not subject himself to the Constitutional Court order that he should present himself to the Zondo Commission to answer allegations about his involvement in state capture.

In addition, since revelations about the looting of VBS Mutual Bank came to light in 2018, the ground seems to be shifting beneath the feet of the EFF and its influential top structure. Newspaper reports were awash with revelations about how some of the money embezzled from the bankrupted VBS Mutual Bank ended up in Malema's accounts through a company linked to the brother of Malema's deputy, Floyd Shivambu. As details became known of how they both splashed out on luxury clothes and vehicles,[60] the EFF suddenly encountered intensely hostile public opinion. The two leaders found themselves being implicated in bankrupting a mutual bank whose clientele was almost exclusively poor, working black communities. The EFF had to explain itself, probably for the first time.

Ironically, Shivambu was greeted in Parliament with the chant the EFF had used against Zuma: 'Pay back the money!'

The EFF's hypocrisy, coming to the fore at the time when the black middle class was most aware of the effect of corruption on their

---

60 Grootes, S. 2020. VBS Bank heist arrests: Who's next? *Daily Maverick*, 18 June 2020. https://www.dailymaverick.co.za/article/2020-06-18-vbs-bank-heist-arrests-whos-next/. Last accessed 14/05/2021.

lives, robbed the party of the spectator support of the middle class, who had earlier enjoyed being entertained by the EFF. The VBS matter showed that, despite their political posturing, the EFF and the ANC still met at the feeding trough.

In 2016 the bank gave Zuma a loan of R7,8 million to reimburse the state for the Nkandla expenses. According to the EFF, VBS Mutual Bank was being victimised (by being put under administration) because of this fact.[61]

The EFF is also experiencing a dilemma where the judiciary is concerned.

The party says it supports the Zondo Commission, but is worried that the commission is too lenient with Gordhan. However, Malema complained vehemently when the commission probed the financial affairs of his controversial Ratanang Trust and subpoenaed banks to provide details of accounts belonging to him, some of his associates and some members of his family.[62]

Because EFF leaders have personal gripes with certain institutions, including law enforcement, the party finds itself having to qualify its position on corruption.

It is clear, then, that the EFF was born of personal squabbles. There has been a long-standing suspicion that the EFF is purely an instrument founded to fight personal legal battles on behalf of a couple of its leaders. This very same aspect could also become the party's biggest millstone.

---

61   African News Agency. 2018. VBS Mutual Bank 'victimised for giving Zuma a loan' – EFF. *IOL*, 11 March 2018. https://www.iol.co.za/business-report/companies/vbs-mutual-bank-victimised-for-giving-zuma-a-loan-eff-13727610. Last accessed 14/05/2021.
62   Jika, T. 2020. 'I don't have anything to hide': Malema as Zondo guns for EFF leader, allies. *TimesLIVE*, 18 October 2020. https://www.timeslive.co.za/sunday-times/news/2020-10-18-i-dont-have-anything-to-hide-malema-as-zondo-guns-for-eff-leader-allies/. Last accessed 14/05/2021.

The EFF has used the genuine challenge of inequality, poverty and destitution experienced by the majority of black people to make hay. And for that, the party has had moderate returns at the ballot box.

The EFF has had relatively good electoral growth in the two elections that it has participated in. In their first showing, in the 2014 national elections, the EFF attained 6,35 per cent of the total vote. The party would increase its share to 10,8 per cent in the 2019 elections, becoming the first opposition party to hold third position for two consecutive elections.

Since the first democratic elections in 1994, no party has held on to the third position in consecutive elections. Smaller political parties have always alternated in this position. Because it has claimed this spot, the only way up for the EFF must be to depose the DA and become the official opposition.

The DA, right now, is not in a position to wage a decent defence, having slipped into an identity crisis that has resulted in a major leadership exodus. Fortunately for the DA, it currently still enjoys double the electoral support that the EFF has (20,77 per cent vs 10,8 per cent in 2019).

The EFF itself is also facing the biggest risk the party has ever faced since its creation. Malema and Shivambu's legal troubles will weigh heavily on the EFF as the single most influential factor on the party's growth prospects. The poor youth, many of them radicalised by the party itself, could become cynical about the EFF.

The big question is whether it can survive the VBS scandal, as well as whether Malema can survive what comes out of the Zondo Commission inquiry into his trust and his activities in Limpopo when he was the president of the ANC Youth League.

For now, however, the EFF finds itself in a moral crisis about the party's position on fighting corruption, and this has to do with the fact that its leaders are personally implicated in benefiting from maladministration. And their defence of deflection and transferring blame is weak and ineffective.

In addition, the sycophancy of the educated EFF leaders around Malema is disheartening. Even the ANC with its warped 'democratic centralism' still seems more democratic than the EFF. ANC members are allowed to express their factional affiliations all over social media and on public platforms. This does not happen in the EFF, and poses a challenge to this party's growth.

For example, the studious support by some senior members of Ace Magashule, the now suspended secretary-general of the ANC, is often shown on social media, in spite of party resolutions against him. Magashule has himself used social media to make a case for the nationalisation of the Reserve Bank, for example – something for which he has been criticised publicly by other senior party members, such as finance minister Tito Mboweni.[63]

One would imagine that South Africa's least offending political party, the DA, would have seized the moment and consolidated its support base. They could have attracted those who are tired of the ANC, and EFF's radical politics. The DA should be on a mission to consolidate moderates by crafting a political project that would do what the EFF and the ANC are failing at: uniting the people of South Africa.

Having come out of the progressive liberal politics of Helen Suzman, the DA is well positioned to pursue multiracial politics aimed at the common good. But the DA has disappointed in this regard. Instead, it opted to recast itself as a party that aims to consolidate the minority vote – the white minority, that is. This brought about

---

63 Jika, T. 2019. The ANC is at war with itself. *Mail & Guardian*, 7 June 2019. https://mg.co.za/article/2019-06-07-00-the-anc-is-at-war-with-itself/. Last accessed 14/05/2021.

the return of Helen Zille as the party's Federal Council chair in 2019.

Before her return, Zille controversially tweeted in 2017 about how the legacy of colonialism in Africa cannot all be negative.[64] At the time, she was premier of the Western Cape. She did not stop there, creating more backlashes as she tweeted about race, racism and apartheid in 2019[65] and again in 2020 – the last time, stating: 'Lol, there are more racist laws today than there were under apartheid. All racist laws are wrong. But permanent victimhood is too highly prized to recognise this.'[66]

As Zille's battles were raging, the DA also resolved that it would not support affirmative action nor use race as a criterion in its policies. This is because the ANC continues to abuse race to justify some of its senseless policies, such as black economic empowerment, according to the DA.

The DA's battle with race and how different race groups dominate the party's policy choices became a heated issue within the party. Internal pressure culminated in a scathing report implicating former party leader Mmusi Maimane, who was heavily criticised for poor leadership after the party's dismal performance in the 2019 elections. For the first time, the DA lost electoral support at the ballot box. The votes the party attained shrank from 22,23 per cent in 2014 to 20,77 per cent in the 2019 national elections, after having grown from 12,37 per cent in 2004 and 16,66 per cent in 2009.

The DA was spooked by its poor performance in the 2019 elec-

---

64 https://twitter.com/i/events/842275216533381120.
65 Tandwa, L. & Karrim, A. 2019. Zille slammed for 'insensitive' tweet on land and race generalisations. News24, 30 December 2019. https://www.news24.com/news24/SouthAfrica/News/zille-slammed-for-insensitive-tweet-i-did-not-compare-land-reform-to-rape-20191230. Last accessed 14/05/2021.
66 Hans, B. & Villette, F. 2020. DA to decide if Zille's apartheid-related tweets breached rules. IOL, 25 June 2020. https://www.iol.co.za/capetimes/news/da-to-decide-if-zilles-apartheid-related-tweets-breached-rules-49885756. Last accessed 14/05/2021.

tions, and Maimane was indeed out of his depth.

I knew at the election centre in Pretoria in 2019 that he would be pushed out of the party. He never got a firm grip on the DA, and had been challenged and criticised as not being the right person to lead it. During his tenure, he was often eclipsed in Parliament by the ever-growling John Steenhuisen, who would ultimately succeed him. Maimane resigned from the DA in October 2019, after Gauteng mayor Herman Mashaba left the party earlier that month. Both Mashaba and Maimane's resignations were triggered by Zille's return to the party.

The elective congress chose Steenhuisen to lead the party. With his ally Zille, Steenhuisen is seen as driving the DA to becoming a white-dominated party.

The report on the election results, drawn up by three prominent party members, stated categorically: 'It is our carefully considered view that the single most important factor in shaping the DA's current circumstances is a failure of effective leadership.'

Some of the key problems, among others, were identified as:

- A lack of clarity about the party's vision and direction.
- Confusion about the party's position on key issues.
- The erosion of the party's unity of purpose.
- Deep divisions within the national caucus.
- A failure to produce a credible policy platform.[67]

The party's response to this, however, was rather concerning. The DA opted to become an identity-based party concerned with farm murders and the negative effect on white people of the ANC's transforma-

---

67 Democratic Alliance. 2019. *A Review of the Democratic Alliance: Final Report*. 19 October 2019.

tion project. This is what some in the DA consider a return to classical liberalism, but the party can only be criticised for its knee-jerk response to its electoral upset in 2019.

Prior to those elections, the party was dealing with genuine concerns about what type of opposition it needed to become to be able to take over the government. The party had shown steady growth and had just breached the 20 per cent ceiling in the 2014 elections. But during Maimane's tenure as the leader of the DA – from 2015 to 2019 – the party struggled to formulate a coherent message or even policy alternatives.

The party was preoccupied with President Jacob Zuma, during whose tenure the opposition had it relatively easy. Zuma kept on giving them fodder that secured a series of court victories against his decisions in government. The opposition became complacent and did not focus much on developing new messages and alternative policies. Opposition parties, especially the DA, had become reactive and not proactive. Once Zuma left office, the cracks within the party were exposed.

Even with the ANC descending into further crisis, with Ramaphosa struggling to stabilise the party, the DA still could not hold up. It failed to grow, despite the disastrous Zuma years. (Even the EFF attained a moderate growth of 4 percentage points.) The DA assumed its support was declining because it was not firm enough in its opposition to the ANC and that it was upsetting the party's traditional constituents.

The party lost further votes, and admitted to that fact, because of the hasty reaction of one of its leaders to a photograph taken in January 2019 of Grade R pupils in a primary school in Schweizer-Reneke in the North West province. It depicted black learners sitting on their own in class; the DA's youth leader, Luyolo Mphithi, denounced it as racist. The teacher, Elana Barkhuizen, was suspended, but the Labour Court later ruled that no racism had taken place. The DA investigated the incident, and a report by the deputy federal chairperson, Refiloe Nt'sekhe, found that this incident had a significant influence on the party's national election results.[68]

As far as I can gather, the DA decided – because of the electoral upset – to abandon the idea of building a progressive multiracial centre upon which to galvanise a majority. Instead of building itself as multiracial party, the DA opted to protect its traditional support base, some of whom were struggling to come to terms with the influx of black leaders.

Ironically, earlier in her tenure as the leader of the DA, Zille had championed the idea of growing the party among black constituents. She actively helped the rise of some black leaders within the organisation, including the party caucus leader Lindiwe Mazibuko and Mmusi Maimane, who would take over from her as party leader.

Having abandoned centre politics and pursued identity politics, the DA's only prospect for forming a government are now by way of a coalition with other minority parties. This is what the DA has experimented with in some key metropolitical municipalities, such as Johannesburg and Tshwane, where the ANC could not attain an outright majority to form a government. More about that later.

Suffice it to say, at this stage some of the DA's coalition partners have caused serious moral dilemmas within the party. For example, the DA-led cooperation agreement with the EFF in the City of Johannesburg certainly spooked hardline DA supporters. The party also

---

68 News24. 2020. 'Racist' Schweizer-Reneke school picture 'could have contributed to' DA voter loss. Politicsweb, 8 March 2020. https://www.politicsweb.co.za/politics/racist-schweizerreneke-school-picture-could-have-c. Last accessed 14/05/2021.

wasn't able to consolidate its power in any of the metros governed by a coalition.

The ANC meddled in these coalitions and the DA had to do whatever it took to keep them going, sometimes entering into agreements that seemed not to make sense in the context of the party's own positions and policies. Some within the DA prefer a focused party making decisions based on principles, as opposed to political expediency and the need to govern. DA supporters did not want the party to become 'ANC Lite'.

From the experience of leading coalition governments in municipalities since the 2016 elections, the DA should have learnt that coalitions with minority parties can come at the cost of having to compromise some of your principles. There is always a risk of entering into agreements with a party whose leaders might face allegations of impropriety. A perfect example is a coalition with the EFF, morally unjustifiable given the DA's relatively clean record and the party's stance on corruption.

In conclusion, the opposition cannot take credit for the ANC's sharp decline in 2019 to below 60 per cent of the votes for the first time. The ruling party's electoral misfortunes were self-created and the opposition cannot be said to have had a hand in it; the opposition is yet to inflict significant damage on the ANC's electoral base.

South Africa's two main opposition parties are experiencing too many internal challenges that are stunting their growth. It is not clear when the opposition will consolidate – perhaps when it is possible for them to enter pre-election coalitions. It took such an agreement between Malawi's opposition parties to depose the ruling party in the 2020 elections, for example.

But the South African opposition is too fragmented to coalesce successfully, and it has become a radicalised space.

The ANC should not rejoice, however. Even with a weakened opposition, it is facing a bleak future and its demise is playing itself out.

EIGHT
How much time does the ANC have left?

Liberation movements typically have a lifespan of about 30 years in government before decay starts to set in. They do not always lose power formally, but more often than not they have to start taking extraordinary measures to stay in power.

Our neighbour Zimbabwe is a case in point. There, the erstwhile liberation movement Zanu-PF has ruled for 41 years. However, to keep its hold on power, the party has had to resort to violence, land seizures and electoral shenanigans. In a fully democratic setting, with free and fair elections, it would likely have been unseated by now.

In South Africa, at the time of writing the ANC had been in government for 27 years and the party was already showing signs of severe fatigue. I believe that within the next ten years it will lose its near-total grip on power, which will have significant implications for how the party will have to organise itself to survive.

The context is that the ANC is highly unlikely to interfere with democratic processes and prolong its stay in power without winning elections fairly. The ANC is learning to live with electoral loss, having lost control of key metros such as Nelson Mandela Bay, Tshwane and Johannesburg at some point. After failing to secure a sufficient majority to form a government in those municipalities, the ANC has democratically disrupted and filibustered the local councils through countless motions of no confidence against coalition governments.

Though obstructive and, at times, a hindrance to smooth governance, this is constitutionally permissible and within the bounds of the law.

There are two ways of looking at the ANC's result in the 2019 election. One is to say that the party's downward slide since its high-water mark of 69,69 per cent in 2004 has hastened, with its support falling by 8 percentage points since the 2014 election. Another is to say that, despite the well-documented corruption and mismanagement of the Zuma years, the party still managed to bag 57 per cent of the vote. In the last scenario, President Cyril Ramaphosa probably deserves a fair share of the credit, meaning that his standing in the party – or at the very least the standing of his faction in the ANC – is vital to its long-term fortunes.

After winning the contentious Nasrec elective conference in 2017, Ramaphosa built a reputation as someone who could implement reforms and rebuild capacity in the public service, despite the divisions in the ANC. Most analysts attached to established financial institutions in South Africa, including the big banks, pushed the idea that even non-ANC supporters should consider voting for the party because that would give Ramaphosa a strong mandate to tackle the internal problems in the ANC and sort out the RET faction. Or so the argument went.

I must confess that I struggled to grasp the logic behind this reasoning and thought it was based more on wishful thinking than anything else. Whenever I pointed out that a bitterly divided ANC was not about to allow its president to rewrite the Nasrec party resolutions because he had helped the party evade electoral disaster, I was chastised for being a prophet of doom. In my discussions with asset managers, I predicted that the ANC would not even acknowledge that Ramaphosa had helped the party through a difficult election, let alone allow him more leverage to manoeuvre behind the scenes. The mandate belongs to the ANC, and not to an individual in the ANC.

But corporate South Africa was buying the idea that a strong mandate would embolden Ramaphosa in the ANC. I held the opposite view: that a strong mandate would make Ramaphosa less useful to the ANC because it would be misinterpreted by the ANC to imply public approval of the party's performance in government. In particular, it would signal to its members that there is no price to pay for rampant corruption and state capture – and that the party could do so again with impunity. The deep structural defects in the ANC cannot be fixed by simply propping up a likeable leader.

Since taking power in 1994, the ANC has had a relatively consequence-free existence, with the party seldom being punished at the ballot box for any missteps in government. Its seemingly guaranteed support has contributed to a certain arrogance in power. When it is pointed out that a particular policy is irrational, the party simply points to its overwhelming electoral support as the basis for the legitimacy of its decisions. 'Might makes right' may be a more apt slogan for the party than 'A better life for all'.

To embolden such a party with another strong mandate would be madness, I thought.

As predicted, the party did not credit Ramaphosa for its performance. Within a week of the May 2019 elections, the line emanating from the ANC was that no individual should be credited above the party. The ANC had carried the day by itself. This portrayal of the election was not surprising. The ANC is – on the surface, at least – about the collective, and not about individual glory.

Stripped of context, the ANC's result in the 2019 elections does not look all that impressive. The drop of nearly 5 percentage points was the biggest swing – in either direction – in the party's fortunes since the 1994 election. After winning 62,65 per cent of the vote in the first democratic elections, the party increased its share by an average of roughly 3,5 percentage points in the two subsequent elections, reaching its high point in 2004 with 69,69 per cent. Thereafter, it dropped roughly 3,7 percentage points in each of the following two elections (2009 and 2014), before the fall of 4,65 percentage points in 2019. Given the background against which the election took place – with the state capture years still fresh in the minds of voters – Ramaphosa actually did fairly well, with a drop that is only slightly worse than the party's average electoral decline since 2004.

The general trend, though, is still unmistakably downwards: two more national elections like the most recent one and the party will dip below 50 per cent overall support.

The downward trend could even accelerate if the ANC's problems become compounded in the coming years, though this is by no means guaranteed. The second possible accelerant is if the opposition parties get their act together, or if an entirely new electoral force emerges, capable of taking the fight to the ANC.

In 2019, the opposition's struggles aided the ANC in limiting the damage of the state capture years. Indeed, one wonders where the opposition might have ended up had it not been for their top vote-getter, one Jacob Gedleyihlekisa Zuma. You might even call him the opposition's 'number one'.

The spectre of Zuma's presidency loomed large over the election, even though he had, by that stage, been out of power for more than a year. The steady stream of revelations about the excesses of the state capture years was still continuing unabated and corruption had decimated capacity in government to the point at which it had an immediate and measurable effect on people's lives. The ANC's own discussion documents were candid about the fact that Zuma was an electoral liability.

Ramaphosa was the party's antidote to the poison of the state capture years. Even his enemies in the ANC realised that they needed him to shepherd the party through the elections. The knives would remain sheathed until after voting day.

In the period leading up to the 2019 elections, Ramaphoria had not yet lost all of its shine and the perception that Ramaphosa could reform both the ANC and government was still quite prevalent – for example, among the banks' analysts mentioned above. The president's track record was not yet long enough for a critical interrogation of this perception. This helped Ramaphosa to limit the ANC's losses to just under 5 percentage points. But within this reprieve lies an implicit covenant with the voters: that Ramaphosa must reform the state and the ANC. This establishes the yardstick against which Ramaphosa, if he is still leader, and the ANC will be measured at the next national elections, in 2024. One would expect that a significant share of voters would demand to see a reformed state and ANC by that time.

A great deal of Ramaphosa's survival hinges on a successful fight against corruption. In this, the ANC can be as much of a hindrance as a help. With its competing factions – one of which benefited handsomely from the Zuma years – the party is simply not wired for a war against graft.

Ramaphosa's detractors have already let rip by implying that the fight against corruption is a smokescreen for settling scores in factional battles. Senior party figures, including Zuma, have accused the judiciary of bias, while others have cast aspersions on the work of the Zondo Commission. Jessie Duarte, acting secretary-general of the party, penned an extraordinary article in which she attacked the commission, claiming that the testimony there was an 'onslaught on the people'. Her subsequent apology to Zondo left few convinced.[69]

---

69 Grootes, S. 2021. Jessie Duarte's onslaught on the Zondo commission, decency and justice. *Daily Maverick*, 9 February 2021. https://www.dailymaverick.co.za/article/2021-02-09-jessie-duartes-onslaught-on-the-zondo-commission-decency-and-justice/. Last accessed 14/05/2021.

These mixed messages coming from senior ANC figures threaten to undermine the ANC's campaign promises to tackle corruption.

If Ramaphosa's enemies win the battle – which, at its heart, is a battle over who controls state institutions – the state's philosophical position about the fight against corruption would have to be altered. If Ramaphosa prevails in his anti-corruption crusade, which entails allowing state institutions to carry out their jobs without political interference, the ANC will eventually change altogether. The impasse must be settled one way or another, because a point of compromise between the two factions about the corruption issue no longer exists.

If the laws of the country are seen by some as unjustifiably pitted against ANC members, a political victory by that group could see those laws overturned or fundamentally alter the way in which they are implemented. This is the reality of what a political victory by the RET faction would entail – retooling the anti-corruption machine so as not 'unjustly' to prosecute those who are aggrieved. If this group succeeds and unseats Ramaphosa, the cost to a country still reeling from the long-term effects of state capture would be huge. This is perhaps also a factor adding to the president's ultra-cautious approach in his own party: one misstep could be ruinous to the country. A victory by a faction made up of senior members facing corruption would, of course, bring a swift end to any illusions about the ANC's ability to 'self-correct' and possibly cripple the party at the ballot box. Without another credible champion of anti-corruption, the ANC will struggle at the next election.

In 2024, the ANC will be reaching the milestone of 30 years in government. The party will probably celebrate it with great fanfare, but it is also the point at which a liberation movement should start looking over its shoulder. If the decline in the ANC's electoral fortunes accelerates, it could fail to win an outright majority. But even if the rate of decline merely keeps pace with that of the past few elections, the party is destined to fall below the 50 per cent mark in 2029.

As we go deeper into the decade, the ANC's proud history fades further away in the rearview mirror. New memories about the theft and plunder of the state capture years are elbowing the old ones out of the way. Younger voters, especially, have no personal recollection of the party's glory years. One way to arrest the decline is to establish a fresh reputation, to tackle corruption and poor governance with the same zeal with which it fought against apartheid. While this transition is not impossible, it is highly unlikely in the current circumstances. Should Ramaphosa not prevail at the ANC's elective conference in 2022, the chances are pretty much nil.

The reprieve and prospects for reform ushered in by Ramaphosa were also undermined by newer revelations that have engulfed some of his allies, removing some of the shine from his anti-corruption crusade. Yet, he still represents to many the last defence against corruption in an ANC government. His defeat in the ANC will be an unequivocal defeat for anti-corruption forces in South Africa. Any leadership that takes over the ANC will find it difficult to make a moral case against corruption, and will drift further away from ordinary citizens.

Whether the ANC will survive 2024 with its absolute majority intact depends, to a large extent, on what Ramaphosa's presidency can achieve in its first term before the elective conference of 2022. I will return to this conference in greater detail later, but for now it is important to highlight that the cynicism that set in as Ramaphosa's presidency unfolded can only be settled by a major shift in the ANC, and that no moderated reforms will achieve this. The picture becomes complex in the sense that the more Ramaphosa achieves what he promised in government – for example, fighting against corruption – the more tensions emerge within the ANC, making it difficult for him to win a second term in the party. That Ramaphosa's anti-corruption drive in the government is creating enemies for him in the party is an open secret. He must fight this battle, since it is the basis upon which the idea of self-correction in the ANC rests; yet the immediate impact is that it unravels the ANC, making it more difficult for Ramaphosa to keep a tight grip on the party.

A political compromise between the factions in the ANC will not look attractive to South Africans, who have already endured a compromise Cabinet under Ramaphosa when he inherited a swathe of Zuma loyalists there and in Parliament. What complicates this further is that a compromise may entail some transgressions not being prosecuted, with implications for the rule of law in the country. A political compromise as a condition for stability aimed at attaining reforms and with no adverse implications for the rule of law would be justifiable. However, the differences between the factions in the ANC render such a compromise impossible because some impropriety must be prosecuted to secure the legitimacy of state institutions.

After promising to fight against corruption and restore confidence in the public service, Ramaphosa finds himself in the midst of a sticky conundrum: on the one hand, he has to manage and contain the mutinous RET faction; on the other, the patience of South Africans is running thin. Ramaphosa cannot take the ANC to the next elections with a message full of promises again; he has to demonstrate at least some victories.

As far as the ANC's internal politics is concerned, his enemies accuse him of allowing special interests to infiltrate the party, having received significant financial support from players in the corporate sector to secure victory at Nasrec.[70] The more state-driven

---

70 Cowan, K. & Tandwa, L. 2019. Exclusive: Leaked emails reveal who Ramaphosa's CR17 campaign asked for money. News24, 3 August 2019. https://www.news24.com/news24/SouthAfrica/News/exclusive-leaked-emails-reveal-who-ramaphosas-cr17-campaign-asked-for-money-20190803. Last accessed 14/05/2021.

anti-corruption measures push out senior ANC leaders such as Ace Magashule, the more Ramaphosa will face criticism from the RET faction that he is hollowing out the ANC.

Survival within the ANC while succeeding in government is a difficult balance for Ramaphosa. When it comes to Ramaphosa's performance in government, including the fight against corruption, the impact inside the ANC and across society is asymmetrical. If the benefits are attained in the state, then the cost is felt in the party in the form of increased tensions. If the benefit is seen in the ANC in terms of unity in the organisation, the cost is felt in the state where decisions – or the lack thereof – do not please the broader public.

There is another way that the ANC could pursue, although the party is not well positioned for this. It is worth exploring with an eye to the future, though. What makes it more unlikely is that this route will not save the ANC from an impending electoral loss in 2024 or 2029. It entails the ANC undergoing a transformation that sees the party being removed from the clutches of the old guard and a new generation of leaders stepping forward who can build a relationship with the increasingly youthful population.

This type of transformation can only be driven by young cadres whose political fortunes are not embedded in the current factionalism that has engulfed the party. It is difficult to imagine the current factions reaching a compromise that would strengthen unity in the party. Theirs has become a zero-sum game, where gains by one faction mean losses by the other. The ANC would have to be rebuilt on the ashes of the current factions and the young cadres in the party must see their destiny beyond factions. This is probably too idealistic an expectation, given the current state of the ANC.

The ANC is also facing another hurdle that has begun to affect the party's outreach to voters. It is struggling with funding, making it difficult for the party to organise election campaigns. With the culture of election campaigns driven by rallies and mass transportation of members to various locations, the drying up of funds has made it difficult for the party to connect with voters in the way that has traditionally been the case with the party since democracy: mass rallies. The Zondo Commission has heard how some of the funds embezzled through government tenders ended up funding ANC activities. The engine of the ANC has, in recent years, been oiled through public funds.[71] It has relied on financiers who tend to benefit directly from government policy, at times to the detriment of the people.

With every revelation of embezzlement that emerges, there is an increased public awareness regarding corruption. South Africans are beginning to learn the truth of the precept 'follow the money'.

Complicating the ANC's finances in the run-up to the 2024 elections is that the party will also have to disclose who its private funders are, making it difficult for the first time for the party to receive funds from controversial donors whose relationship with the party may have been kept secret in the past. This follows an edict from the Constitutional Court that the law should be amended to compel disclosure of private party funding. The campaign for greater disclosure of private funding dates back many years. The ANC had for a long time resisted passing laws that compelled disclosure of campaign financing. It took fifteen years for the Constitutional Court to come to grips with the issue and rule that the disclosure of private funding is mandatory. As an incumbent, the ANC has used its control of public resources to channel some of the money to the party. The party established an investment company,

---

71 Southall, R. 2008. ANC for sale? Money, morality & business in South Africa. *Review of African Political Economy*, 35(116): 281–299.

Chancellor House, responsible for raising funds for the ANC. Chancellor House has been a beneficiary of government expenditure[72] for building power plants, among other things. With the new law in place, it will be known to voters who the ANC's funders are, and who may be expecting to gain from the decisions of the party in government. All of this creates an unfamiliar electoral environment for the ANC, compounded by the problem of a general decline in electoral support, a trend that has been in place since the 2009 election.

Besides the new law that constrains fundraising for the ANC, the party is also facing uncertainties about how the independent parliamentary candidates will affect its electoral share. The ANC has thus far not favoured electoral reform, believing it would undermine the party and loosen the party's hold on its members. As such, it has poured cold water on suggestions to introduce the constituency system for parliamentary seats. But, a small NGO called the New Nation Movement (mentioned in Chapter 6), changed all that. In 2020, it succeeded with its petition to the Constitutional Court to compel electoral reforms to allow independent candidates to run for parliamentary seats without having to stand on a party ticket.

It is still unclear precisely what a new electoral system would look like, but this much is clear: a scenario in which individuals can hold a seat in Parliament without having to account to a party is not one that the ANC favours, as can be seen from the vehemence with which it has opposed a constituency system in the past. The new law would have to be in place prior to the 2024 elections. The court

---

72 De Wet, P. & Mataboge, M. 2015. Chancellor House: R266 m for nine years of lies by ANC partner. *Mail & Guardian*, 29 September 2015. https://mg.co.za/article/2015-09-29-chancellor-house-r266-million-for-9-years-of-lies-by-anc-partner/. Last accessed 14/05/2021.

ordered Parliament to pass new regulations within two years[73] – in other words, by June 2022. The law may encourage some party members who believe the ANC has lost its moral compass to abandon the party and stand as independent candidates, as we have seen in municipal elections where this practice is allowed. In municipalities, the independent candidates have in some instances destabilised the ANC's hold on power, as many have defected from the party.

The shift in terms of electoral reforms as driven through litigation creates electoral uncertainty for the ANC, and the party has no experience of operating in such an environment. This will throw up hurdles for the party in the 2024 elections, compounded by the party's ongoing struggle to craft a believable message for voters.

A significant number of ANC voters have begun abandoning the party, although they have not always shown an eagerness to embrace the opposition parties. Many disgruntled ANC voters simply stayed home in 2019. Although the party's share of the national vote only fell by just under 5 percentage points, its number of raw votes declined by 12 per cent compared to 2014. All told, the ANC lost 1,4 million votes between 2014 and 2019. The DA itself lost 400 000 votes, so it is unlikely that they gained a huge chunk of the ANC's missing 1,4 million. The biggest beneficiary was clearly the EFF, which gained just over 700 000 votes compared to the previous election – but even that is not enough to account for all of the ANC's losses.

As 2024 comes closer, the pressure on the party intensifies. It is too stretched – financially and culturally – to manage the situation

---

73 Du Plessis, C, 2020. Experts wrestle with the nature of changes to South Africa's electoral system. *Daily Maverick*, 17 August 2020. https://www.dailymaverick.co.za/article/2020-08-17-experts-wrestle-with-the-nature-of-changes-to-south-africas-electoral-system/. Last accessed 14/05/2021.

and turn things around in a short space of time. Internal divisions are yet to reach a climax and conflicts are escalating in the build-up to the next elective conference of the party, in 2022, where Ramaphosa will seek a second term as leader. The ANC's fall, whether it comes in 2024 or 2029, would not be attributable to a single factor but to all of these factors coming together to create a perfect storm.

It is always worth keeping in mind that the ANC's decline since 2004 has been gradual rather than rapid: a 3 per cent drop here, a 5 per cent fall there.

The giant has been almost counted out before, only to awaken from its slumber and show surprising resilience with a hard core of loyalist supporters undergirding it. But, just like old age, its decline is inexorable and undeniable. The only question is how fast it will progress.

The ANC has weakened not only electorally since its high point in 2004 but also institutionally. Internal differences in the party have hardened into starkly opposing and irreconcilable world views on how the state, its economy and its politics ought to be organised. Resolving this is improbable without a major correction that will split the party.

Should the ANC fail to win an outright majority in either the 2024 or 2029 elections, it will likely still be the biggest party, with the strongest prospects of forming a coalition government. It will likely be spoiled for coalition partners, depending on who leads the party or which faction has prevailed.

Failure by the ANC to secure an outright majority would also have implications for how the party relates to other centres of power across a more decentralised state, where no single party holds absolute sway.

It is highly unlikely, for example, that the ANC would immediately lose control of all eight provinces where it currently governs.

Provinces have their own dynamics, and these dynamics do not immediately apply to the national sphere. In some provinces, such as Limpopo, the ANC might remain strong, which may encourage regionalisation of the party, with local centres of power used as a platform to dominate national party leadership. With stronger regions, the ANC at national level could begin to look more like a federal council – ironic, given the party's general distaste for federalism, but nonetheless highly likely if the above scenario does play out.

In the next chapter, we look in greater detail at how the ANC could be reconfigured if it fails to secure an outright majority in either 2024 or 2029.

By the end of the decade, at the ripe old age of 117, the giant may have to learn a few new tricks.

NINE
The morning after Election Day 2029

When one is accustomed to standing on the highest mountain, being merely king of the hill can feel like a massive climb-down.

This is the scenario awaiting the ANC in the not too distant future. The party that has ruled South Africa unchallenged for nearly three decades faces the prospect of losing its grip on absolute power – if not in the 2024 elections, then before the end of the decade in 2029.

Even if it dips below the 50 per cent required for an absolute majority in the National Assembly, it is highly likely that the ANC would still emerge as the largest party in the next two elections. Despite its declining trajectory, the party has a hard bedrock of support that acts as a buffer against any party trying to surpass it.

Equally, it is highly likely that the ANC would still rule the roost in a large number of provinces – probably even the majority of provinces – even if it loses national control. There are several provinces where the ANC enjoys a much larger buffer than on the national level. In the 2019 election, the ANC received 57,5 per cent of the national vote, leaving it with a margin of error of 7,5 percentage points. In many provinces, it is much further away from falling below the key 50 per cent threshold. For example, in Limpopo, the ANC received a full three quarters (75,49 per cent) of the votes for the provincial legislature. Other provinces where the party is still sitting pretty, despite some slippage since its heyday, are:

- Mpumalanga: 70,58 per cent;
- Eastern Cape: 68,74 per cent;
- North West: 61,87 per cent; and
- Free State: 61,14 per cent.

In the Northern Cape, the ANC's performance almost exactly mirrored its national showing, with the party receiving 57,54 per cent of the votes for the provincial legislature. Prior to the 2019 elections, the opposition had high hopes for the province. With more favourable demographics for the DA than many of the other rurally dominated provinces, it seemed like an inviting target. It is one of only three provinces where support for the ANC has ever dropped below 50 per cent (in 1994, when the party received just a whisker under 50 per cent of the votes). But although support for the ANC dropped by nearly 7 percentage points – more than the national average – the party still secured a comfortable enough majority.

Should the ANC fall below 50 per cent nationally, however, one would expect this domino to fall as well – especially as the party's drop-off in the Northern Cape outpaced its national decline during the 2019 elections.

KwaZulu-Natal is another province where the ANC fell by more than the national average. It was perhaps the only province where the absence of former president Jacob Zuma hurt the party. Besides the Western Cape and the Northern Cape, it is the only province where the ANC has ever fallen below 50 per cent. In 2019, the party's share of the KZN vote dropped by 10 percentage points compared to 2014, leaving it with 54,22 per cent of the provincial vote. It will also be a prime target for the opposition parties in the 2024 election – or, failing that, in 2029.

In the Western Cape, the ANC has never received an absolute majority, and Gauteng is already hanging by a thread after the party squeaked home with 50,19 per cent of the votes for the legislature in 2019.

In the above scenario, the ANC would end up controlling five of the nine provinces outright, in addition to being the largest party in the National Assembly. Nothing to sneeze at, but if you've spent three decades wielding near-absolute power, it would be a fairly rude awakening to this state of affairs on the morning after Election Day 2029.

When the initial shock wears off, the party will need to plan its next step – perhaps after some recriminations about how it reached this point. The first priority would be to find coalition partners on the national level and in the provincial legislatures where it won a plurality of votes but not more than 50 per cent of the seats.

As the giant descends from the mountaintop, he will likely find an eager array of suitors waiting below. But, as in life, a political marriage entails an element of compromise.

Until now, the ANC could do pretty much as it pleased on the policy front. Any criticism of its plans could be swatted away by pointing to its overwhelming victories at the polls and riding roughshod over any attempts to thwart its agenda in the National Assembly and the provincial legislatures. Only the courts and independent institutions such as the Public Protector could sometimes act as a brake on the party's worst instincts.

But entering a coalition means some form of compromise, diluting the ANC's central control over government policy. The extent of the compromise will likely depend on how far below the 50 per cent mark the party ends up.

An intriguing scenario in which the ANC is just one or two seats shy of an absolute majority in 2024 is not beyond the realm of possibility. In such a scenario, one of the country's many tiny parties could gain outsize influence by putting the ANC over the top.

In a later chapter, we will look in more detail at the question of coalitions and likely partners for the ANC, but suffice it to say that this is one of many areas where the ANC would have to adapt in the event of a setback at the ballot box.

If the ANC fails to retain its outright majority in Parliament, the cake will become smaller for party members on a national level, opening the door for provincial structures of the party to emerge as stronger power centres.

The party's 'personality' will also be affected. As its grip on the levers of government loosens and its power is dispersed over a wider area, the ANC's national identity will weaken and become more fragmented.

To use a current example, a large part of the DA's identity is tied to its power base in the Western Cape, where it leads the provincial government, the Cape Town metro and a host of smaller municipalities across the province. The DA was able to build on its reputation for competent governance in the Western Cape to make gains in other provinces. 'Let us do for you what we did for the Western Cape,' was the underlying theme of the party's message to despairing voters in areas crippled by years of neglect and municipal mismanagement. The party, realising how important the Western Cape was to its national fortunes, often deployed its best people in provincial posts. As party leader, Helen Zille famously – and somewhat controversially – chose the premiership of the Western Cape over a seat in Parliament, where she would have been the official leader of the opposition in the National Assembly. She realised that the DA's success in the Western Cape was crucial to its ability to win votes elsewhere.

Unfortunately for the DA, the sword cuts both ways. As part of its policy of deploying top party officials to key local and provincial government posts, it had elevated Patricia de Lille, former leader of the Independent Democrats, to the Cape Town mayorship in 2011. De Lille held the post for several years, until things started to go horribly wrong in 2017. Her relationship with the DA's top brass broke down irretrievably amid disciplinary charges and motions of no confidence in her mayorship, culminating in De Lille stepping down as mayor in October 2018 and resigning from the party.

The extremely messy divorce tarnished the party's image not only in the Western Cape but also nationwide, one of many factors contributing to its decline in the 2019 elections. The De Lille drama undermined one of the DA's key selling points: that it was the party of competent government, not hamstrung by constant internal squabbles like the ANC.

Unlike the DA, the ANC's image is mostly shaped by its actions in national government – and the ruling party has preferred it that way. In this, it has been aided by the fact that our country does not have particularly strong devolution of powers from the national government to the provincial and local spheres. If a party gets the bit between the teeth, like the DA in the Western Cape, it can still effect real change on a provincial level, but if the political will is absent, it is easy for provincial structures just to coast along and take the lead from national government.

This has certainly been the case for the ANC, which has a strong tradition of centralised decision-making in the party. But without domination at national level, it would lack a critical platform to express and consolidate its national identity.

The ANC's governing philosophy holds that any weakening of the national sphere of government as a centre of power would have a detrimental effect on its ability to influence the direction of society. The party's long-standing fear of losing control of provincial and local spheres of government is already partly being realised – even before it has lost total national control. This is due to a combination of factors, including the poor performance and ill-discipline of members deployed in local government and outright electoral defeat in areas where the party once held sway, such as the big metropolitan municipalities of Tshwane, Johannesburg and Nelson Mandela Bay.

As the party wanes at the national level, it would have little choice but to adapt in line with this pattern of its decline, thus becoming a party with stronger regions. If the scenario sketched at the beginning of this chapter plays out, the ANC would retain an outright majority in five provinces – something it would lack on the national level. This would strengthen the ANC regions in those provinces. Additionally, it could still control a large number of municipalities outright, even in provinces where it fell short of the 50 per cent threshold. Since the party is not declining equally across the country, its regionalisation will look different in different areas. Saying there will be 'nine ANCs' is putting it too strongly, but the party will become more fragmented after either 2024 or 2029.

With the ANC losing support in urban centres, the question that refuses to go away is whether it is irrevocably on its way to becoming a rural party.[74] Leon Schreiber made this observation in his book, *Coalition Country* (2018). The ANC will most likely consolidate power where the party still enjoys electoral domination, and rural support has been the party's bulwark since 1994. The five provinces in which it has a good chance of retaining control, even in a scenario where it dips below 50 per cent nationally, are provinces in which a significant part of the population still lives in rural areas. The municipal results of 2016 also point to a party declining faster in urban areas (such as Tshwane, Johannesburg and Nelson Mandela Bay) than in its rural heartland.

---

74 The Conversation. 2016. The ANC remains dominant despite shifts in support base. BusinessTech, 3 August 2016. https://businesstech.co.za/news/government/132309/the-anc-remains-dominant-despite-shifts-in-support-base/. Last accessed 14/05/2021.

However, this not a straightforward phenomenon, as we will see in a later chapter focused on the nature of the rural voter, and there are ways for the ANC to remain a regionally strong party without necessarily becoming a rural party.

The ANC becoming a more regionalised party also has implications for how the party reconfigures itself at central leadership level. Increased input and influence from ground-level regional members could even have a healthy effect on the ANC's centralised leadership culture.

Currently, the ANC's NEC is dominated by members serving at national level in both government and party. ANC policy discussions are also dominated by members serving at national level. The arrangement of democratic centralism within the ANC requires that branches and regional structures of the party are 'consulted' in the process of policy formulation, but this is often just a smokescreen. Regional members are urged to show discipline and not challenge the decisions of the party's national leaders.

Political scientist Tom Lodge has pointed out that so-called consultative decision-making in the ANC is hampered by 'ineffective structures'.[75]

ANC leaders at national level have become accustomed to making decisions without consulting with the membership of the party across branches and regions, or to otherwise just making a show of consultation when the result has been preordained.

This has increased tension between leaders in government and the activist rank-and-file membership of the party. Regarding the fissure between the central leadership and these members in provincial and local structures, Lodge notes that 'to retain political office leaders will pursue gradualist programmes, and whilst doing

---

[75] Lodge, T. 2004. The ANC and the development of party politics in modern South Africa. *Journal of Modern African Studies*, 42(2): 189–219, p. 198.

so will seek to restrain their rank and file and limit the scope of democratic procedures within their organizations'.[76]

Gradually, the consultation with the rank and file of the party on key policy decisions within the ANC is becoming a matter of referendum and not a discussion on policy matters. In recent years, delegations from branches to conferences have been elected based on their willingness to stick to a particular position instead of their desire to engage with ideas and find a compromise.

As mentioned earlier, the ANC has historically been suspicious of federalism, believing that it would promote tribalism and undermine attempts to forge a unified South African identity. But if the party's decline at national level unravels its organisational structure and culture, it could force the party to rethink greater devolution of power to the regions. It could also reignite the national debate about federalism in a South African context. As the ANC becomes more regionalised and fragmented, the party may become a reluctant federal party to survive.

The history of South Africa – political domination at national level coupled with some form of self-governance – has meant limited influence of regional and local identities on the primary political identities of the majority of citizens. Thus, local and provincial governments are seen as spheres of delivery of material services, as opposed to spheres of expression of political identities.

This is what separates the ANC from the DA in relation to national and sub-national spheres of government. The DA favours a stronger system of federalism and prefers more autonomy for local and provincial government.[77] Besides using the Western Cape to

---

76 Ibid.
77 Inman, RP & Rubinfeld, D. 2009. *Federalism and South Africa's Democratic Bargain: The Zuma Challenge*. Berkeley Program in Law and Economics, Working Paper Series. https://www.law.berkeley.edu/files/Zuma.pdf. Last accessed 14/05/2021.

showcase its ability to govern successfully, the province is also where the primary political identities for the majority of DA supporters are formed. These voters feel no affinity for the national political identity, which has thus far been shaped by the dominant ANC. The DA's experiment in the Western Cape shows that, if regional government performs, it can be a source of primary political identities for citizens. The discussion about how Americans relate to their federal government (central government in the South African context) as opposed to their state and local government (provinces and municipalities in the case of South Africa) is quite instructive in imagining how the ANC would adapt to the dispersion of power from national to sub-national spheres of government.

If we agree that the human quest for self-determination is the same everywhere, despite different institutional arrangements that may impede or encourage it, then the way in which Americans have related to the devolution of powers across national and sub-national spheres of government could have a bearing on the debate in South Africa.

The constitutional scholar Alan Tarr makes the point that political identities are not fixed, but often shift over time: 'Among federal systems, there are some in which citizens' primary attachment is national and their secondary attachment is to the constituent unit, and some in which the attachments are reversed. In other federations the situation may be more complicated. It is possible that the primary political identity of citizens may change over time, as has occurred in the United States – one should not consider people's perceptions of their identity as a fixed and unambiguous preference set.'[78]

---

78 Tarr, A. 2013. Federalism and identity: Reflections on the American system. *L'Europe en Formation*, 369: 20–38.

When it comes to democratic experience, no country on the African continent is closer to mimicking the American system than South Africa. South Africa loves to copy America, while reserving its right to repudiate America's foreign policy and some of its values. Having lived in both societies, I find their politics more comparable to ours than has been acknowledged, despite the anti-American rhetoric in South Africa and the occasional dressing-down of South African politicians by the American establishment. The comparison between the two countries in terms of how political parties have navigated the flow of power across national and local spheres is warranted.

Regardless of the ANC's emphasis on national identity, South Africa is a diverse country with plenty of room for regional identities to assert themselves. The apartheid government used a divide-and-rule strategy to split groups along their regional identities, such as ethnicity. This is why the ANC was suspicious of any kind of federal arrangement that would maintain the regional identities of the apartheid system, particularly ethnic identities. This fear was quite palpable in the period leading to the transition in the early 1990s, with political violence in Gauteng and KwaZulu-Natal taking centre stage.

The ANC's concerns back then had merit, given the deep ethnic divisions that could have undermined the process of building a united South Africa. Three decades later, the political landscape looks quite different, and regional identities do not have to be feared, particularly if political identities have evolved and changed over a period of time, as Tarr argues in the context of America. Regional political identities need not be permanent identities based on ethnicity. They can also be built on other factors, including development objectives.

Another hard reality to which the ANC will awaken following a failure to win an outright national majority is that the party will suddenly have less patronage to dispense. For a party that has been feeding at the government trough for three decades, that will be quite the adjustment. Electoral decline will necessitate coalitions at the national level, meaning the party would have to entice potential partners with some key positions in government, reducing the ANC's flow of patronage and largesse to key figures in the regions and branches.

Thus, the party's decline will weaken the grip that the national leadership has on its branches and regional chapters. In some respects, the process has already begun, with the central leadership starting to lose control of branches and leagues. The phenomenon can no longer be explained away as merely an expression of internal robustness within the party. Different decisions and positions taken by the ANC leagues and some of its provincial chapters are difficult to reconcile with the party's position. For example, a decision by the national leadership that party members facing charges of corruption should step aside was not accepted by all the leagues and provincial structures.

Although much of this is instigated by sinister factional elements vying for power at the national level of the party, the drifting away of the regions and branches from the central leadership of the party can probably no longer be reversed, even if one imagines the (unlikely) end of factionalism in the party. The ANC regions are starting to become more and more autonomous in their thinking. While the ANC remained hegemonic and dominated the policy discourse in the country, the provinces, regions and leagues toed the line and seldom dared to challenge the national leadership of the party. Now, the ANC has no option but to contend with more autonomous party regions.

These multiple centres of power will have a profound impact on

South African politics. A provincial chapter of the ANC would naturally prefer to consolidate its power in a province by organising itself along the demands of its constituents, as opposed to diktats from the central leadership of the party. What the ANC would require to survive and remain in power in Limpopo province might be different from what is required for the party's survival in KwaZulu Natal, for example. As coalitions become more common, the ANC might have to be flexible about some of its ideological positions to accommodate its partners. At regional level, the focus of the party might be more pragmatic than ideological.

The ANC can survive as a regionalised party without necessarily being reduced to a rural party. It is necessary to draw a simple distinction between a political party that is stronger across regions and yet weaker or loosely organised at central level, and a party that is only stronger in rural regions.

If we consider that the ANC would learn to survive despite the decline of power at national level, it makes sense that the party may consolidate power to dominate regions across the country, thus becoming a federal party. Regional politics would require that the party builds a strong constituency network through which regional leaders have a direct relationship with the constituents. This naturally disperses power from the central leadership of the party to regions. If regions are to survive, they have to forge new and honest relationships with constituents, entirely different from the cadreship culture that has characterised how the ANC dominates its branches. The ANC would have to undergo transformation from below at regional level, based on the need to survive and remain in power across regions.

South Africa's democracy is evolving towards decentralisation, and the ANC has been unable to push back successfully against this. The litigation-driven electoral reform will also create a favourable environment for further decentralisation of power, allowing for independent candidates to stand for parliamentary positions.

In the period leading to the 2016 municipal elections, the ANC in Gauteng had difficulty in explaining why Jacob Zuma's face was not on the party's election campaign posters.[79] The provincial leadership was seen as breaking ranks with the national leadership of the party. Beneath the squabble is a deeper issue relating to how the ANC in Gauteng had to balance its identity as the region demanded. The Gauteng electorate was very attuned to the corruption and state capture issues, which meant that the ANC in the province needed to yield to that. That placed the ANC in Gauteng in defiance of the national leadership, which preferred to make Zuma the face of the campaign, despite the cloud of corruption allegations hanging over his administration. The ANC in Gauteng felt it could only survive if it defined itself clearly against corruption, with or without the approval of the central leadership of the party. E-tolls is another issue on which the Gauteng ANC staked out its own path – bowing to pressure from its constituents in the province, who detest the system.

To survive in the long term, the ANC in Gauteng would probably need to become even more autonomous as a region. Its sharp decline in the 2019 provincial election, and the results in Johannesburg and Tshwane in the 2016 municipal elections, a warning shot.

In the same manner that Gauteng has already started to distance itself from the national ANC, the party's other regions will also have to identify and respond to the issues close to the hearts of its constituents. In Gauteng, it was corruption and e-tolls; in a province like

---

79 News24Wire. 2016. ANC explains why Zuma's face is not on election posters. *BusinessTech*, 2 June 2016. https://businesstech.co.za/news/government/125477/anc-explains-why-zumas-face-is-not-on-election-posters/. Last accessed 14/05/2021.

the Free State, it could be municipal service delivery, which all but collapsed when the province became one of the looters' prime hunting grounds during the state capture years.

The ANC is increasingly likely to face an electoral environment that is unfavourable to the party's organisational culture of democratic centralism. For ANC regions to survive in an electoral environment leaning towards a strong constituency system, the party will have to reform its branch structures to encourage meaningful participation in democratic processes.

The possibility of staying in power at regional level – through either an outright majority in a legislature or a provincial coalition – will likely discourage breakaway parties. Regions will prefer to remain under the same brand as the ANC, but they will offer a different menu to attract voters in each province – in much the same way as McDonald's offers a Boerie Burger in South Africa, a Shrimp Burger in South Korea and a McKroket in the Netherlands.

TEN

The coalition conundrum

A liberal democracy is in essence a multiparty system – for which the South African Constitution makes provision.

Our political system must be based on values such as 'universal adult suffrage, a national common voters' roll, regular elections and a multi-party system of democratic government, to ensure accountability, responsiveness and openness'.[80]

In such a system there needs to be legislative provisions[81] for participation by a multiplicity of political parties in elections, as well as in decision-making processes. It is not only about the delivery of tangible returns for voters; it is also about the extent to which people are involved in the process and in decision-making about service delivery.

In a multiparty democracy the resultant policy decisions are presumed to be more legitimate than outcomes that have been decided on by the majority without consultation with other parties. The presumption is also that a policy decided upon through consultation will most likely be more rational.

It is easy quite simply to judge a country's political system by checking whether it has laws that allow for the existence of oppo-

---

80 Constitution of the Republic of South Africa, Act 108 of 1996, Section 1(d).
81 Matlosa, K. 1992. Multi-partyism versus democracy in southern Africa: 'Whither Lesotho'. *Law and Politics in Africa, Asia and Latin America*, 25(3): 327–340.

sition parties, and which allow them to participate in political processes. However, the picture changes when actual participation by those parties in influencing political decisions is used as an additional yardstick.

The political scientist Robert Dahl famously argued that a multiparty democracy exists when an opposition party wins elections twice consecutively. However, in Africa, very few democracies will pass his requirement of a power exchange. In the southern African region, power exchanges have been rare in the past 25 years, with one recent exception being the case of Malawi, where an opposition coalition successfully unseated the long-time ruling party.

According to Dahl's requirement, this should mean that the southern African region has weaker democracies – a sentiment that is gaining traction as an explanation for the current threats to democratic consolidation in South Africa.

South Africa does have a multiparty system, with opposition parties represented in national, provincial and local spheres of government. However, no opposition party has won a national election since the first democratic elections in 1994. The ruling party continues to dominate politics and has more than twice the political support enjoyed by the biggest opposition party, the DA. However, the ANC's support on the national level has been declining and could possibly even drop below the necessary majority level required to form a government. In fact, one could say that the ANC has, over the past three decades, squandered its political capital.

As mentioned earlier, after securing a total of 62,65 per cent of votes in 1994, the party's support initially grew to 66,35 per cent in 1999 and a massive 69,69 per cent in 2004, but since then has steadily declined: 65,9 per cent (2009), 62,15 per cent (2014) and 57,5 per cent (2019).

There is little doubt that the ANC is experiencing a crisis because of its descent into corruption and the abuse of its strong hold on the country's policy direction to benefit the party's patrons.

But South Africa's disaffection with the ANC is also proof that voters are becoming increasingly sceptical about a system dominated by a single party. South Africa has never benefited from any possible advantages of this system. There hasn't been robust and smooth policy making, nor implementation, since a titan does not have to commit to lengthy consultations with anyone else.

An even greater negative effect of the party's dominance of the political landscape is the fact that serious internal divisions in the ANC have crippled policy progress in government – much more than any consultation process with the opposition ever could have. On top of that, Jacob Zuma's tenure as president has shown that such a system can easily be captured by outside interest groups.

Does the solution to this problem then lie in a coalition government? If indeed South Africa is experiencing a policy deadlock and general poor performance under a system in which one party dominates, could the country reverse this by entering a phase of coalition governing at national level? If so, what would these coalitions ideally look like and what else could they achieve if they were to be formed in the current political setting, prior to the 2024 national elections?

There is a real prospect of seeing a coalition government after those elections.

Unfortunately, our recent local experience with coalitions has not bolstered our trust in such a system.

The country's first important experience in this regard was with DA-led coalition governments at sub-national level: on provincial and metropolitan tiers. The party entered into a coalition with smaller parties to lead a coalition government in the City of Cape Town Metropolitan Municipality after the 2006 municipal elections in which no political party attained sufficient majority to form a government. In subsequent elections, the party increased its majority, governing without the need for a coalition.

In 2009, in the national and provincial elections the DA also took control of the Western Cape provincial government. Eventually, since taking over the province on more than one level, the DA has become the dominant party in the region – creating another system in which one party dominates, and negating important lessons about coalitions we could have learnt.

Looking at possible post-ANC coalition governments, it is obvious that the DA will have a big influence on such a structure, but the reality is that, where it cannot dominate, the party has a poor record of managing coalitions. This is because the DA has been struggling with how to position itself as a coalition partner. Judging by the way in which the DA has presented itself since the party was taken over by Helen Zille and John Steenhuisen, the DA seems unsure whether to present itself as the bigger party that would influence the agenda of the coalition, or as a participant in a coalition where parties have more equitable representation.

If, indeed, the DA manages to consolidate a minority coalition with progressive partners, it could face the reality of having to compromise by returning to the centre on certain matters.

The DA has shifted its electoral strategy since Zille's return to lead the party's Federal Council. It has shown itself as no longer interested in building a democratic centre where parties coalesce around issues that concern them. The DA's actions since the 2019 elections have given tons of ammunition to those who accuse the party of concerning itself primarily with the interests of the white minority. This is an electoral niche in which the Freedom Front Plus has cemented its hold by lobbying on behalf of white Afrikaners.

When I wrote an opinion article in December 2020 on News24 in which I criticised the DA for being seduced by identity politics, the party's spokesperson replied by stating that the DA still embraces the progressive centre and still aims to build a political majority made up of different races.[82]

However, at its policy conference in 2020, the DA resolved to do away with race-based redress,[83] citing how the policy has been abused by the ANC. This is where the DA gets it wrong. The party seems to conclude that whatever the ANC has failed in is of no further interest to South Africans. By doing away with race-based redress as a guiding principle in public policy, the DA has abandoned a common agenda on which a progressive majority could be built.

The media red-flagged the DA's 'race denial', but while this debate was still raging, the party announced it was going to campaign against farm murders – a hot-button issue for many white voters.

Leon Schreiber states in *Coalition Country* that he does not view the DA as a troubled potential coalition partner. It makes for a perfect coalition member, since its inclusion would advance democracy.

However, not all coalitions are useful in democratic advancement. And much has changed within the DA since I sat down with Schreiber at the Franschhoek Literary Festival in 2019 where we discussed his ideas about the future of coalitions and the role of the DA, the party in which he now serves as an MP. Since then, the

---

82 Mbhele, Z. 2020. Right of reply: The DA has not abandoned politics. News24, 12 December 2020. https://www.news24.com/news24/columnists/guestcolumn/right-of-reply-the-da-has-not-abandoned-centre-politics-20201212. Last accessed 14/05/2021.

83 Gerber, J. 2020. Policy preference: DA leaves race out of redress equation. News24, 5 September 2020. https://www.news24.com/news24/southafrica/news/policy-conference-da-leaves-race-out-of-redress-equation-20200905. Last accessed 14/05/2021.

DA has abandoned the idea of building a majority from the centre; it is receding towards minority politics, which are ideologically unfavourable to a functional coalition.

In addition, in a society that has deep ethnic and racial cleavages, coalitions are faced with rigid political identities. Race and ethnicity as policy foundations are non-negotiable and they become the albatross around the neck of any possible compromise environment that is required to sustain coalitions. People can compromise on temporary identities but not on permanent ones.

There must be common ground for coalitions to work, and they should also advance democracy according to liberal principles.

The two dominant opposition parties will most certainly be the most influential, outside the ANC, when it comes to the direction and lifespan of any national coalition. However, they are not well-aligned to contribute to a progressive coalition.

The DA and the EFF have nothing in common except the need to remove the ANC from power. Beyond that, it is not clear how they can proceed to make decisions in government. This is a big challenge to the opposition camp; it is too fragmented to form proper coalitions.

At the end of the day, we are left with an ANC-dominated coalition, which will not necessarily advance democratic values. If the ANC enters into a coalition with the EFF, the two parties will see their co-operation as an expression of the will of the grand majority, but in reality they will be ignoring the fact that voters did not wish to give either of them an outright mandate to govern.

But let's consider the relationship between the EFF and the ANC.

The EFF is an extreme leftist nationalist party, priding itself on being solely concerned with the well-being of black people, in spite of the Constitution encouraging a multiracial democracy based on shared values. The EFF believes that only black people are entitled to govern and make key decisions in society. Its leader, Julius Malema, has been hauled to court many times to answer charges of hate speech and inciting violence against white people.[84] His party has also repeatedly made it clear that it is not interested in liberal consensus politics. Can the EFF, as third-biggest party in the country, become a reliable coalition partner? Experience suggests that the answer is no.

The 2016 municipal elections catapulted the party to the position of 'kingmaker' after the ANC failed to win an outright majority in the City of Tshwane, City of Johannesburg and Nelson Mandela Bay Metro. What took place in those hung local governments as attempts were made to create governing coalitions was a disaster. And the EFF was always on the scene. For example, it entered into a 'voting agreement' with the DA that would allow the latter to form governments in Tshwane and Johannesburg. However, the EFF did not want to govern with the DA and therefore did not support the very DA-led government it had helped put into power.

The EFF would subsequently disrupt these DA-led coalitions, collapsing both in Tshwane and Johannesburg.

It also put forward policy ultimatums and brought up issues that had nothing to do with local government or a specific municipality. For example, the EFF would threaten to pull out of the coalition with the DA because the latter continued to support the state of Israel and its occupation of Palestine.[85] The EFF did not even recognise that it

---

84 Head, T. 2020. Malema faces new 'hate speech' case – and he may do battle with Gerrie Nel. *The South African*, 13 December 2020. https://www.thesouthafrican.com/news/what-new-hate-speech-julius-malema-gerrie-nel-court-afriforum/. Last accessed 14/05/2021.

85 Mitchley, A. 2017. Malema calls for cutting all ties with 'apartheid' Israel. News24, 2 November 2017. https://www.news24.com/news24/southafrica/news/malema-calls-for-cutting-all-ties-with-apartheid-israel-20171102. Last accessed 14/05/2021.

had entered into coalitions with the DA in Tshwane and Johannesburg. It said that it had only agreed to a 'voting agreement' to ensure the removal of the ANC from power.

This raises serious doubts about the EFF's possible contributions towards a progressive coalition at central government level.

Coalitions cannot be based solely on a common enemy; they need to be driven by the objective to arrive at shared goals. The coalitions that involved the EFF have crumbled. In fact, the party eventually orchestrated the removal of the DA-led coalition in Tshwane and helped install an ANC-backed coalition – further proof that this coalition was never based on principle but was simply a case of elite power bargaining. Such bargaining, not guided by shared principles, does not serve the interests of the people.

Coalitions are often referred to as 'elite pacts', implying that voters are usually not directly consulted when coalitions are entered into. If party leaders are then seen to abuse their mandate, and if they enter into coalitions that do not advance a discernible and defensible political agenda, the coalition will crumble. This does not mean that the parties must always agree, but they should be genuine in their intentions and hopefully also seek to advance democratic values as well.

South Africa therefore needs to shift towards a multiparty system in both spirit and practice. The ANC's dominance over the past three decades has ensured that this has not happened. There is, however, noticeable pressure from below (by opposition parties and NGOs) in this direction and the ANC is unable to stop it.

This is an important feature of our political scenario, since political parties tend to misunderstand why nations arrive at coalition governments. Because parties choose such a government in an effort to ensure that they get their share of the power pie, their leaders tend to think coalitions are completely authored by parties.

However, it works the other way around: when voters withdraw their support from a dominant party, the message is that (1) they do not trust their votes to be in one place where those votes would create an overly strong political mandate; and that (2) they do not want to entrust their votes to the specific dominant party. A signal is therefore sent from below that parties no longer need a grand majority to make decisions and implement policy on voters' behalf, to which the opposition parties react.

But to embrace multiparty governance and a coalition system would require a complete shift of attitudes towards co-governance. Not all coalition governments will deliver on all aspects. Some will deliver on material services to the people while coming up short on consultation, or vice versa. What matters the most are the immediate reasons why a coalition is needed, as in South Africa at present, where the political crisis can be turned around by a progressive coalition aimed at uniting people and not one based on elite power bargaining.

Even unstable coalitions can yield democratic dividends by moving towards a culture of transparency and consultation in policy making. This has been the missing ingredient under the ANC, which has finalised policies and taken resolutions in the party with little meaningful consultation with the public.

Therefore, despite the main opposition parties being poor candidates for an effective and stable coalition government, such a structure may still be the answer to address the political crisis created by the ANC.

However, let us be clear about what it can achieve.

If the intention is to introduce a culture of policy making in which a multitude of parties are involved, a coalition government could set the scene for that. Coalitions, however, will not speed up service delivery, nor will they speed up the process of decision-making. But they can provide greater governmental legitimacy and a stronger mandate to policy makers. Coalitions coming after a political crisis can restore citizens' trust in the political system and may strengthen the culture of consultation.

Countries that need a coalition government as badly as South Africa does are inevitably already struggling with making a success of a liberal democracy. They will also struggle with coalition forming and may experience instabilities that appear worse than under a system in which single party dominates.

However, the instabilities inherent in a coalition are a problem that the country can live with, compared to the political crisis of stagnation experienced in a scenario dominated by the ANC. Coalition governments are often defined as inherently unstable. It need not be so. They could be a source of legitimacy. They could also gradually introduce critical changes to the political culture, as well as increased consultation during the policy-making process.

In our case, it could break the policy deadlocks so often seen under the current system. A coalition government's policy making could also be restricted by delays, but it cannot be worse than what is being experienced under the dominant ANC where deadlocks are often brought about by divisions within the party and the tripartite alliance.

Coalitions will set the country on a long-term trajectory of a shift in political culture, as parties embrace the idea of co-governance. Even singular positive outcomes will strengthen the position of the coalition. For example, if the resultant cooperation puts a brake on rampant fruitless expenditure in public service, yet fails to expedite rapid economic development and policy implementation due to a deadlock among its partners, the coalition would still have succeeded in the greater scheme of things.

Coalitions are not perfect, and they do not always serve all purposes at the same time.

But South Africa desperately needs to shift towards consensus-driven policy making to restore public trust in the system. If a coalition introduces equitable bargaining on policy, then it will serve a good purpose. Most importantly, the long-term democratic dividends of a coalition can be a better governed society with a more stable political party system.

Sure, South Africa will go through a teething process and will learn much along the way – which could result in a period of instability. As it evolves, however, a coalition can improve the democracy by dispersing power across multiple centres, instead of centring it in one place. This will enhance accountability and the performance of the political system.

ELEVEN

Is there a soft spot in the ANC's hard core?

As the political tides shift in South Africa, washing away the ANC's softest support, one rock has stood strong: a hard core of support in the rural areas of the country. The crashing waves do erode the rock, but it is slow change, spanning many years.

In the two decades from 1999 to 2019, the ANC's share of the vote in the Eastern Cape fell by only 5,06 percentage points, from 73,80 per cent to 68,74 per cent. In the Northern Cape, its decline was equally modest, with a drop of just 6,78 percentage points over the 20 years. The Eastern and Northern Cape are demographically very different, but what they do have in common is a large rural population.

Contrast this with the urban hub of Gauteng, where support for the ANC plummeted by nearly 18 percentage points from 1999 to 2019. The results in municipal elections confirm the trend, with the ANC losing control of three big metros, Johannesburg, Tshwane and Nelson Mandela Bay, in 2016. In Cape Town, it has been out of power for more than a decade.

Rural voters are often stigmatised as conservative, backward and less sophisticated than their urban counterparts. They are unfairly characterised as politically naive, with no appreciation of a modern liberal democracy. The tendency to stereotype rural voters is not limited to South Africa. In the USA, for example, coastal elites love to typify rural Americans as gun-toting, Bible-bashing rednecks.

In South Africa, rural areas are associated with a conservative political culture. It is often taken for granted that voters in these areas will vote for the ANC 'until Jesus comes', to borrow former president Jacob Zuma's phrase. Traditional leadership authorities, one of the oldest institutions in Africa, still hold great influence in certain rural areas.

Opposition parties such as the DA and even the EFF have struggled to make inroads into the ANC's rural heartland. When one listens carefully to the views of urban residents, one gets a sense that they blame rural areas for overwhelmingly voting for the ANC.

Despite all this, it would be a mistake to assume that rural support for the ANC will last forever. Limpopo was the ANC's strongest province in the previous election, with the party gaining 75,49 per cent of the votes for the provincial legislature. An impressive number, to be sure, but still 12,8 percentage points less than 20 years ago.

It is also worth keeping in mind that the opposition parties do not need to halve the ANC's rural support to force it under 50 per cent nationally. They merely need to carve off a bigger sliver than they are currently doing. They probably are in need of a sharper knife, though.

One of the biggest factors that could hasten the decline of the ANC's support in rural areas is the shocking state of local municipalities. This is, of course, a nationwide problem, but rural areas have borne the brunt, having been criminally underserviced since the first democratic local government elections in 1996. So the problem is not new. But, as the last vestiges of legacy infrastructure have been stripped away, the situation is becoming more dire, undermining the credibility of the ANC in rural areas.

With the situation worsening apace, it is an overly simplistic analysis to say that rural voters never punished the ANC for poor service delivery in the past, so they will never punish it for this in future.

As can be seen in the above example of Limpopo, the rural vote is not quite as static as the popular imagination believes it to be. It evolves along with other changes in society, albeit sometimes at a slower rate.

Our rural areas have always been intertwined with urban centres. During the apartheid years, the government saw these areas as labour reserves, with the urban centres as industrial hubs and areas of economic activity. This led to the establishment of the migrant labour system. Black South Africans who worked in urban centres were not allowed to maintain a permanent place of residency in those areas, so they always maintained a link to their rural homelands.

Today, the migrant labour system is long gone, but the umbilical cord between urban and rural areas has not been cut. Many black South Africans still maintain a home in rural areas even if they have places of residency in the cities where they work.

So, while rural communities may have a political culture which differs from that of urban areas, they are not totally disconnected from the economic hubs. As urbanisation picks up pace, the economies of the rural areas have begun to rely more and more on staying in close contact with family members and friends who have moved to the city. This allows urban political and cultural influences to spill over to the rural sphere.

There is a widely held perception that rural voters stick with the ANC because they fear an end to the system of social grants if another party takes over. I don't know how true this is, but there is nothing wrong with a community voting for the party it believes will look after its interests the best. The onus is on another party to convince them otherwise.

The hard reality is that many rural voters choose the ANC simply because they do not see a viable alternative. For them, the ANC is the party that brought them liberation, as well as basic services such as electricity and running water. That is why a total collapse of municipal services could be the catalyst for a change in rural voting behaviour. It would undermine one of the ANC's selling points. But for meaningful change to happen, the opposition parties will also have to up their game. Currently, they are very urban-focused, as an investment of limited resources in a densely populated city is likely to yield a better overall return than an investment of similar size in a sparsely populated rural area. However, as opposition support in certain urban areas becomes more entrenched and reaches saturation point, that equation may change.

While the opposition parties have struggled to launch convincing campaigns to win over rural voters, the ANC has benefited from a branch network that stretches into every part of the country. Simply put, the ANC is just more visible in these areas.

With the exception of the church, the ANC is probably the most ubiquitous private organisation in the rural areas. By contrast, the country's relatively small opposition has to spread itself much more thinly and is less present in these areas. Voters literally do not 'see' an alternative to the ANC. The culture of participation in community gatherings, or *lekgotlas*, is alive and well and the ANC is usually a strong presence there.

Many communities in the rural areas still fall under traditional leadership authorities, which operate alongside a civilian local government structure. The ANC mostly has a cordial relationship with these structures, and they are allowed to coexist with a democratic system without clear delineation of responsibilities. The ANC has cut an implicit deal with these authorities: we allow you to run your affairs and your land with a minimum of interference, while you enable us to harvest votes in your area. Most traditional leadership councils work closely with ANC governments. With their financial sustainability dependent on a government allocation, most traditional leaders realise the consequences of challenging the ANC. As for the opposition, they have a much tougher task getting access to voters staying in the areas under traditional authority.

The country's traditional leaders are often embroiled in controversies, ranging from the splashing of money by royal houses to disputes about the legitimacy of certain local chiefs. All these have to be mediated by government through policy, so the institutions of traditional leadership are beholden to the ANC government. But there comes a point at which government performs so poorly that not even persuasion by traditional authorities could persuade voters to stay with the ANC. In this scenario, certain traditional leaders who feel that the ANC has usurped some of their powers, despite their informal alliance, might not put up that much of a fight.

The service delivery backlog in rural areas and the general lack of infrastructure has already led to traditional leaders reclaiming some of their powers and taking active steps to govern their communities, a phenomenon that I described at length in my previous book.[86]

Since the dawn of democracy, the ANC has to some extent displaced traditional leaders, who had powers to govern locally under apartheid. With a new local government system, elected government is responsible for development. This nearly soured the relationship between government and traditional authorities,[87] and has been a point of contention in restructuring local government in South Africa.

---

86 Mathekga, R. 2018. *Ramaphosa's Turn*. Cape Town: Tafelberg.
87 Rugege, S. 2003. Traditional leadership and its future role in governance. *Law, Democracy & Development*, 7(2): 171–200.

Far from being politically naive, rural communities understand the need to tackle their concerns through institutions, and traditional authorities have been filling the institutional gap created by a failing local government system.

Another concern for the ANC under a possible new electoral system is that rural areas might gravitate towards independent parliamentary candidates who emerge from their areas. With the ANC's legitimacy crumbling even in the eyes of traditional authorities, this can create a viable environment for a strong constituency system in rural areas. For the first time, rural communities could feel there is a viable alternative available to the ANC.

The possible introduction of a constituency system could fundamentally alter the nature of the rural vote and activate local leaders who have grown disgruntled with the ANC and other political parties. The ANC would have to start working harder to earn the votes of rural voters.

As the ANC becomes more fragmented and decentralised, an opportunity for a rural-focused political party might present itself. Such a party may focus on the shared development challenges confronted by rural communities across a specific province, or perhaps even the country.

An underappreciated aspect of the ANC's strength in the rural areas is that it is in many ways a by-product of its pro-poor policies. Since many rural voters are also poor, the rural areas have been receptive to these messages. ANC policies, for the most part, do not reflect any great bias in favour of rural areas. Therefore, it is not unthinkable that a political party that focuses on rural regions (as both a living and an economic space) may interest communities that for a long time have only been engaged on the basis of their poverty.

In this manner, the decline of the ANC at national level could reignite a locally based approach to development, allowing for a politics that caters for regions and is less concerned with the centre. Having been neglected in terms of development, many rural areas share common concerns, meaning that they are ripe to be targeted as a group by a new political organisation built around their needs – for example, a party with a strong focus on farming, the main economic activity in the rural areas and one of the few sectors of the South African economy that occasionally shows decent growth.

Politics, like nature, abhors a vacuum and nowhere is the vacuum greater than in the country's rural areas. Currently, they are caught in a policy haze between traditional authorities and the vote-hungry ANC.

If one takes the time to travel across rural areas in South Africa, one is struck by the significant real estate development in certain areas. The investment in housing by private citizens in rural areas is quite impressive and could amount to billions – except that no one knows the value of the property owned by the residents of rural areas. This is because many of these residents do not own the land upon which they built their houses.

The houses that are built in rural areas are often not evaluated since they are not built on land with title deeds. The land is usually owned by traditional authorities and the ANC government has not clarified this situation. It is ridiculous that one of the biggest forms of investment, building a house, is not recognised as an economic activity when it takes place in a rural area where there are no title deeds. I often discuss with executives in financial institutions how much value is lost to the economy simply because we decided we are not going to count houses built in rural areas on land without title deeds.

It speaks to the failure of the political system in South Africa that, in the third decade of democracy, the government has not sufficiently addressed the issue of title deeds in rural areas under traditional authorities. People in rural communities often struggle, therefore, to get a mortgage to purchase a house.

To address some of the issues that are quite specific to rural areas, political parties or representatives might ride a political ticket that talks about this conundrum. These are issues that have nothing to do with ethnicity, but everything to do with the extension of security of tenure to rural communities as the people of South Africa. One of the many shortcomings in the country's policy framework is a bias towards urbanisation. The idea that the destiny of the society lies in urban centres has undermined rural areas in terms of development and delivery of services. The policy focus tends to lack potency regarding rebuilding rural areas into centres of economic activity and prosperity.

Another point of policy neglect – another vacuum – relates to the ongoing debate about land reform. The government's controversial decision to go ahead with expropriation of land without compensation will most likely affect rural communities the most. Yet, the debate about land reform has not placed rural areas at the centre of the policy discourse. A rural-based political party could address such an issue in a much more intimate way than has been the case thus far.

Mobilising support based on regional identities was politically taboo during the early years of South Africa's transition to democracy. This fear was rooted in the realities of the apartheid years when the white minority government demarcated rural areas along ethnic or language identities, creating divided communities that were easy to rule.

Nearly three decades since the dawn of democracy, ethnic divisions still raise their heads, as could be seen in the Vuwani case in

Limpopo[88] when a community refused to be demarcated under a municipality that they saw as being controlled by a different ethnic group. But, overall, ethnic divisions are less problematic than they were in 1994. Rural areas are dynamic, and they have development challenges that can be tackled by distinct political parties without having to resort to mobilising around ethnicity or other divisive aspects.

One political party that has embraced rural and regional politics is the Inkatha Freedom Party (IFP), which has its power base in the rural vote in KwaZulu-Natal. The party is still hamstrung by allegations that its leaders perpetrated ethnic killings in the period leading to the transition to democracy in the early 1990s. The controversial history of the IFP somewhat unfairly tarnishes the whole concept of regional and rural-dominant political parties in South Africa. Looking at how rural areas have evolved thus far – amid policy neglect from central government – rural votes will become sufficiently distinct to inspire focused political mobilisation.

If there is any part of the country that requires policy innovation in terms of economic activity, it should be rural areas. Development challenges that have emerged in these areas should inspire new political mobilisation. This is in line with the idea that political power will disperse from the central government to regions as the ANC's total grip on national power weakens. As political power disperses, so will economic activity. There is an opportunity to turn rural areas around and stimulate economic activity in these regions.

The first step that needs to be taken to bring rural areas back

---

88 Tau, P. 2020. Vuwani divided over boycott of municipality as lack of delivery becomes 'unbearable', *City Press*, 15 May 2020. https://www.news24.com/citypress/news/vuwani-divided-over-boycott-of-municipality-20200314. Last accessed 14/05/2021.

onto the economic grid is to tackle the title deed situation discussed above, and the second is to gain an understanding of the true nature of the subsistence economy that dominates rural areas in South Africa. This will give us an indication of how much wealth is tied to the subsistence economy and how value can be unlocked to drive investment in rural communities. South Africa has relatively little knowledge and hard data about this sector of the economy, and this remains a missed opportunity. At this point the major economic developments in rural areas are centred on the construction of shopping malls. Building a retail sector with no other value-adding economic activities can hardly be said to be an investment. While urbanisation continues its rapid rise, there are nonetheless also certain areas in rural communities that have bucked the trend by expanding, and this needs to be reflected in policy.

What does the future hold for rural areas politically? I believe they are ripe to enter a new era of intense political competition if they present themselves as new centres of power. This is based on the hypothesis that political power will disperse from the centre to the regions as the ANC's national influence wanes. This will encourage the formation of multiple centres of political power, and rural areas will be a part of that. It requires that political parties rethink their strategies regarding rural areas.

Thanks to its strong branch network, the ANC has become deeply embedded in the fabric of rural life. To unravel it will no doubt be a time-consuming task requiring patience. But if the opposition is willing to abandon superficial stereotypes about rural residents and pursue an innovative political strategy, they might find that the ANC heartland does offer some fertile ground, after all.

TWELVE

The homeless middle class

It was the ancient Greek philosopher Aristotle who first highlighted the middle class as an ingredient crucial to the success of a democracy – his preferred political system.

Generally, the middle class is defined as the 'middle income' group in society. The benefit of having such a class of citizens was provided by Aristotle in the ground-breaking work *Politics*:

> Wherefore the city which is composed of the middle-class citizens is the best governed; they are, as we say, the natural elements of the state. And this is the class of citizens that is the most secure in the state, for they do not, like the poor, covet their neighbours' goods, nor do others covet theirs, as the poor covets the goods of the rich . . . Thus, it manifests itself that the best political community is formed by citizens in the middle class, and that those states are likely to be well administered, in which the middle class is large, and larger if possible than both the other classes . . . For the addition of the middle class turns the scale and prevents either of the extremes from being dominant.[89]

---

89 Aristotle. 2000. *Politics*, translated by Benjamin Jowett. New York: Dover Thrift Editions.

Aristotle's idea of what a stable, well-governed society looks like remains valid to this day. The existence of a strong middle class and how it relates to the other two classes in the society (that is, the rich and the poor) is a good indicator of the strength of a democracy.

He made it clear that its size is of critical importance. The larger the middle class, the less tension there will be between the poor and the rich. Its presence will also lead to aspiration among members of the poor class – they will believe that they can advance to the 'higher' group with its accompanying benefits. If they entertain such hopes, the tension between poor and rich decreases and the former will be less likely to disrupt the system. The middle class is essentially the glue that holds society together.

If we apply Aristotle's thinking to our situation, where does that leave us? Does South Africa have a large enough middle class to fulfil this mediating role in society? The answer is no, in large part because of apartheid policies that deliberately impoverished the majority of the population, robbing them of economic opportunities that in turn prohibited them from migrating to a higher economic class.

Despite being categorised as a middle-income country, South Africa has a rather small middle class. And only the economic advancement of black people will increase the size of that group.

South Africa is made up of two major classes and they are directly related to race. On the one hand, there is a large poor class, consisting predominantly of black people, while on the other hand there is a small class of rich people, most of whom are white.

One of the reasons for South Africa's relatively small middle class is that not enough poor black people have been given the chance to enter it for South Africa to have democratic stability. And only appropriate policies on the economy and industry will provide economic opportunities for the larger part of the population to become part of the middle-income group.

The homeless middle class

With South Africa's poor economic performance, the middle class has not grown to the desired level.

According to research by the Southern Africa Labour and Development Research Unit, '50% of South Africans are chronically poor. In 2019, only 20% of South Africans belonged to the stable middle class, whilst 4% belonged to the elite. The rest belonged to the transient poor (11%) and the vulnerable middle class (15%).'[90]

With the stable middle class measured at 20 per cent and the rich elite at 4 per cent, this means that over 70 per cent of South Africans are somewhat poor. And for a stable society, as Aristotle argued, the middle class should be larger.

In addition, if the majority of citizens are poor, it creates a burden on the political system, creating social tension that threatens some of the basic principles of a liberal democracy: political tolerance and its ability to find solutions. South Africa's economic fabric – in terms of income distribution across classes – creates a tension-prone policy environment.

That, unfortunately, puts us in a Catch-22 situation, since you need a stable society to make the implementation of certain measures easier – but you will only have a stable environment if there is equitable distribution of opportunities. Only then are shared goals pursued. Groups or classes can coalesce and be brought together in pursuing common goals. The challenge is that, for democracy to be sustainable, some basic social and economic arrangements ought to be in place. To put it differently, a nation should be at a certain level of development to be able to sustain democracy.

In my political studies, I have long grappled with this dilemma.

---

90 Mamacos, E, 2019. Is your family poor, middle class or rich? Find out here. News24, 29 August 2019. https://www.news24.com/parent/family/relationships/is-your-family-poor-middle-class-or-rich-take-this-test-and-find-out-20190821. Last accessed 14/05/2021.

Political scientist Adam Przeworski, who lectured in New York University's politics department, champions the idea that poor countries often struggle to sustain democratic consolidation. Przeworski argues persuasively that poor countries will battle with democracy.[91] His argument is that the poor tend to see democracy instrumentally and they will find it difficult to support certain democratic principles if those principles are not seen to improve their living conditions immediately.

Where the poor make up the largest numbers and the middle class is smaller, the policy discourse will reflect the conflict between classes.

This coincides, then, with Aristotle's view that if the relationship between all three classes is unbalanced and they do not find common ground, conflict will reign as compromises are difficult to reach. A growing middle class will assert itself in society and mediate conflict between the other two. If not, any policy that the rich can benefit from is seen as taking away from the poor, and vice versa.

South Africa is a glaringly obvious example of this, where the absence of a formidable middle class is a serious threat to democracy – particularly liberal democracy. Political participation is driven largely by two dominant classes – the poor and the rich – with the tiny middle class observing. That is why South Africa's policy discourse is increasingly shifting away from compromise politics as the country becomes more unequal. The policy environment has become a zero-sum game between the poor and the rich, in the absence of that all-important buffer between them.

Take, for example, the decision to go ahead with the expropriation of land without compensation. It is seen by the rich as an attack on

---

91 Prezworski, A. 2008. *Poverty, Participation and Democracy.* Cambridge: Cambridge University Press.

their property rights, and by those on the other side of the fence as a justifiable way to help the poor and the vulnerable. The policy is shaped in such a way that gains by the poor would have to impose a loss upon the rich. In this situation, it becomes difficult to expect the poor to defend the principle of property rights. They do not see any prospect of ever enjoying those rights themselves any other way.

This ties in with that all-important solution to reduce the tension between the well-off and the poor: to supply the latter with a realistic prospect of belonging to the middle class.

It becomes clear, then, that in order to de-escalate the tension between the poor and rich, which threatens to erode democratic cooperation, deliberate efforts must be made to grow the middle class through public policy.

The ANC government has not focused sufficiently on doing this. Rather, it has maintained the historical scenario that led to the poor and the rich dominating the discourse. The party has attempted to deracialise capital through its black economic empowerment project while trying to keep the wolf of poverty from the door. But it has no known project to grow the middle class. In fact, the ANC's hold on policy making in post-apartheid South Africa has largely been sustained by the conflict between the rich and the poor. And the existence of a formidable middle class will, without a doubt, threaten the ANC's power base. In the meantime, it courts the poor (for votes) while managing the rich (for income).

Beyond extracting tax from them, the ANC has largely ignored the middle class. In South Africa, empathy with the middle class is tantamount to betrayal of the poor. It is almost taboo to say the middle class is heavily taxed and they pay twice for most of the services they receive from the state.

For example, the middle class pays for public services, such as education and security, through taxes, only to purchase a similar service from the private sector because taxpayer-funded services are poorly delivered. Members of the middle class are the top consumers of private education since the quality of public education keeps on declining. The same can be said about security; the middle class is concentrated in urban areas where an army of private security companies caters for their protection. Homes and properties in urban areas are also barricaded behind high security walls that have become a big expense for households. This is unsustainable, and is adding to the unfavourable conditions for this class.

And yet South Africa has no political party that manages to capture the imagination of both the black and the white middle class. Political campaigns that focus primarily on the plight of the poor often focus on a single issue, and rightfully so.

Despite being headed by a mix of educated middle-class members itself, the ANC does not shape its political strategy to involve the middle class. Indeed, the party seems to see the growth of the black middle class in post-apartheid South Africa as a threat to its own hegemony.

The middle class tends to be more highly educated, more inquisitive, better informed. As voters, its members are complex and multidimensional. They may, for example, vote based on taxation and how tax is spent, making them hostile to increases in social spending. They are also more repulsed by corruption, feeling it is their large contributions that are being abused. They also have better access to information than members of the poor class.

The black middle class, which makes up the greater portion of the middle class in South Africa, has not had a cordial relationship with the ANC. They are portrayed as ungrateful beneficiaries of ANC transformation policies. Zuma even coined the term 'clever blacks' to mock informed black voters who keep on rejecting the ANC in most big metros – as shown in the 2016 municipal elections.[92]

And in provincial elections in Gauteng, where most members of the black middle class are based, the same can be seen. In 2009, the party received 64,04 per cent of the votes for the provincial legislature; after its support decreased to 53,59 per cent in 2014, it eventually nosedived to 50,19 per cent in 2019.

Senior ANC members do not see allies in the middle class.

I was once a guest on a Johannesburg-based radio talk show when the ANC's current acting secretary-general Jessie Duarte called in to the studio. Instead of addressing some of the matters I had raised about the troubled internal processes of the ANC, Duarte started attacking me – characterising me as an out-of-touch middle-class person who lives in a leafy Johannesburg suburb. The implication was that someone like me has no moral standing to challenge the ANC. It is often clear to me, listening to discussions by senior ANC leaders, that they believe that only they have a genuine connection with the poor. And that relationship need not be tainted by fantasies about the middle class.

The ANC's idea of 'our people' is to the exclusion of white people and the middle class, despite the idea of the party being a broad church for all.

The EFF has always been clear that its primary concern is the poor black majority.

The DA has, to be fair, attempted to position itself as a political refuge for South Africa's increasingly ignored middle class.

It was under Helen Zille's leadership that the DA made concerted efforts to attract the middle class across all races. As a party that

---

92 BusinessTech. 2016. Clever blacks exact revenge on Zuma – analyst. 8 August 2016. https://businesstech.co.za/news/trending/132736/clever-blacks-exact-their-revenge-on-zuma/. Last accessed 14/05/2021.

has traditionally relied on the white vote, the DA made efforts to attract black voters, particularly the black middle class. Zille recruited black people to the party leadership, including Lindiwe Mazibuko, Mmusi Maimane and Herman Mashaba. They gave the DA the face of a party that is acceptable to the black affluent class. However, after the departure of all three of these black leaders, as well as a host of other leaders at provincial level, the DA is failing to present itself as a truly multiracial party. When the DA decided it would no longer consider race as a factor when making policy decisions,[93] it effectively abandoned a portion of the black middle class.

This brings us to one of the misconceptions about this important group of voters – the idea that they stand against ANC policies, that they would tag after anything and anyone that opposes the ANC. The reality is that the middle class is not intractably opposed to ANC policies; it is more concerned about the way in which the ANC goes about implementing them.

The black middle class appreciates progressive politics, including some of the policies that the ruling party has adopted. Attempts to attract their vote have been less than robust and show a lack of appreciation of their role in a democracy. The complexity of this class of citizens is also not appreciated. For a local party to rely on the middle class as a distinct voter base, it would need to do a great deal of work to devise political projects that would attract them.

However, in a country like South Africa, with only a small fraction of the population categorised as middle class, there is relatively little reward for any party in targeting middle-class votes. The immediate returns appear not to be worth the effort.

---

93 At its policy conference, the DA decided to do away with race as a criterion when it comes to designing public policy. The policy is fully discussed in the party's policy documents. See https://www.da.org.za/2020/09/the-media-shows-its-racist-underbelly-in-its-portrayal-of-black-da-leaders. Last accessed 31/05/2021.

What it boils down to is that, despite the reality that the middle class is set to grow as the country advances both economically and in democratic consolidation, parties are not conscious enough of the black middle class in particular – which, in turn, leads to these voters being without meaningful influence. At this point, the middle class is caught between increasing political tensions between the rich and the poor.

A struggling ANC does not yet see any benefit in building a sustainable middle class, nor in shaping a strong relationship with the existing one.

The middle class is still awaiting a political home.

THIRTEEN
The Rubicon conference

Before the 2024 general election, another date dominates the South African political calendar: December 2022, when the ANC will once again engage in its five-yearly ritual of electing a new leadership.

After the drama – some would say miracle – of Nasrec 2017, it is almost guaranteed that the latest episode of the ANC's internal *Game of Thrones* will have South Africans glued to their seats. Will President Cyril Ramaphosa survive the trial by combat? Or will the RET faction regroup under the leadership of a new champion after its previous flag-bearer, Nkosazana Dlamini-Zuma, was vanquished at Nasrec?

A week is a long time in politics, the saying goes. In the ANC, it is an eternity.

Analysts are generally on much safer ground making predictions about South Africa's macropolitical trends than trying to speculate about the inner workings of the ANC. The party's internal politics are a treacherous mix of horse-trading, conniving and backstabbing.

Who, for example, could have predicted the manner of Ramaphosa's victory in December 2017: a last-minute deal with Mpumalanga kingpin David Mabuza, until then thought to be a solid ally of the Zuma faction, to prevail by the narrowest of margins in the final vote?

Nonetheless, there are some predictions that we can make with relative certainty.

Ramaphosa is likely to enter the conference holding the moral high ground, having had a large measure of success in placing key institutions such as the NPA and SARS on a solid footing after the devastation of the state capture years. Of course, holding the moral high ground is no guarantee of victory, especially if your opponents are willing to fight dirty, but it remains an important piece of the December 2022 puzzle – even if we won't be able to assemble the full picture for some time.

Regarding the reforming of the ANC, Ramaphosa has moved much more slowly than on the state level, but his careful strategy did eventually bear fruit with the suspensions of secretary-general Ace Magashule, his most prominent rival in the party, and former North West premier Supra Mahumapelo.

It would, however, be a mistake to count the RET faction out. In today's ultra-divided ANC, it is possible to subdue one's enemies for a period of time, but total victory for one faction or another is a tall order. Ramaphosa could very well enter the 2022 conference as the leader of the strongest faction in the ANC, but he is highly unlikely to enter it as the leader of a united party.

The sharp divisions in the ANC have meant that Ramaphosa's state-level reforms have raced ahead of his party-level reforms. Instead of the ANC leading the state, the state is dragging the ANC, kicking and screaming, in the right direction. The eventual suspension of Magashule, for example, was triggered by corruption charges lodged against him by the NPA, which is once again a relatively well-functioning state institution after being gutted during the Zuma years. Despite what the RET faction and its Twitter army would have us believe, there is zero evidence that the charges against Magashule were in any way politically motivated. But they did have a definite political impact when Magashule was forced to step aside. In this manner, Ramaphosa's governmental reforms also bore fruit on a political level – even though there is no indication that this was his motivation.

Ramaphosa and his allies have shown that they are able to work around any ANC recalcitrance in their attempts to re-establish the rule of law. While his enemies still enjoy influence in the party structures, Ramaphosa has used the power of the presidency to drive through important parts of his agenda, though by no means all of it.

Despite enduring a political backlash in the ANC over his anti-corruption crusade, Ramaphosa has been able to expose the moral weakness of his detractors. This enables him to enter the next elective conference on the right side of the dividing line running through the ANC.

The RET faction, which includes Jacob Zuma, Magashule and Mahumapelo, is struggling to paint its crusade against Ramaphosa as a morally justifiable battle. Rather, they have to hope that enough senior ANC members become frustrated with their loss of position and patronage to make a revolution possible. As South Africa is still visibly ravaged by the corruption of the state capture years, as well as by chronic unemployment, the RET faction has very little room to launch a successful fight against Ramaphosa's corruption-busting efforts. The script that Zuma wrote at the 52nd National Conference of the ANC, held in Polokwane in December 2007, is unlikely to work again in 2022. Back then, Zuma successfully staged a political campaign against the institutions of law and order, anchoring his presidency on an anti-establishment platform that also entailed attacking the judiciary and the courts, and infiltrating the prosecutions agency. With the country much more attuned to the destructive effect of corruption, such an agenda would cripple the party ahead of the 2024 elections.

The next elective conference of the ANC will in part be a referendum on what kind of party it wants to be: a party of corruption-busters or a party of rent-seekers. When it comes to the moral battle, Ramaphosa is already a winner, even if he should be politically defeated. He wants both a moral and a political victory, while his detractors are looking for one thing and one thing only: a political victory in the form of Ramaphosa's removal. A political victory without a moral victory, however, would spell trouble at the ballot box. If the ANC needed Ramaphosa to survive the 2019 provincial and national elections, the party would certainly need someone like him to survive the 2024 elections.

The moral dimension at play here works in Ramaphosa's favour. What Ramaphosa ought to emphasise at the next elective conference is the danger of any political decision that lacks a moral basis. By turning up the heat on corruption in state institutions, Ramaphosa is setting the ANC on an irreversible course of confronting the ills that have been accumulated in the party and the state over the past decade.

This renders certain people unelectable unless the party is set on the imminent loss of power. The next elective conference would have to pronounce, clearly, the direction the party will take regarding anti-corruption measures. Other issues are peripheral. If Ramaphosa intensifies his anti-corruption campaign in state institutions – and succeeds – the ANC will have a tough time rejecting him. Ramaphosa's leadership has pushed the party into a corner, where it is faced with a choice.

Despite criticism in the party about the impact of his war on corruption, Ramaphosa has not relented. Institutions that are part of the state's anti-corruption apparatus have been strengthened. In his State of the Nation address in February 2021, Ramaphosa announced the establishment of a new independent statutory anti-corruption body. Ramaphosa's Minister of Finance, Tito Mboweni, allocated a further R1,8 billion to the Department of Justice and

Constitutional Development to 'fight against crime and corruption'.

Ramaphosa is clearly staking his political future on this issue ahead of the December 2022 conference. It is also one of the main issues upon which the electorate will judge him.

The president does not bring much to the table regarding economic success. In this area, he has been less adept at finding a way to sidestep the ANC's influence, even as he has undeniably restored credible leadership at the National Treasury. His rivals, on the other hand, will come to the next elective conference preaching the gospel of economic emancipation. They will likely avoid the question of corruption, except when they retort that Ramaphosa and his allies are manipulating the anti-corruption drive to pursue a political agenda: the purging of progressives in the ANC.

Ramaphosa has thus far decided not to confront his rivals directly on economic issues. He has been more compromising on economic policy direction, resigning himself to the mild idea of incremental fiscal consolidation. Therefore, the differences in the ANC involving the economy are not as stark as the tensions about the anti-corruption campaign. Compromises about conflicting economic positions in the ANC can be reached; however, a compromise about the effect of anti-corruption measures on the political fortunes of some senior members of the party is difficult to imagine, given the potential voter fallout if compromised party members do not have to face the music. Nothing ever has hardened relations among ANC members more than Ramaphosa's anti-corruption agenda.

Ramaphosa was fully aware of the dangers that this agenda posed to his future leadership in the party, but he also realised that compromising about this issue entailed its own risks at the ballot box and in terms of damage to his own reputation. The clampdown on patronage and nepotism has had a direct effect on the pockets of certain members who were part of the rent-seeking faction during the Zuma years. In the end, it is money that lies at the heart of the most vehement internal opposition to Ramaphosa.

Unlike the Nasrec conference, the next elective conference will not offer the ANC the option of choosing the middle ground on the corruption issue. At Nasrec, Ramaphosa's victory provided respite for those who believed the party needed a fresh start after the Zuma years. On the other hand, the broader leadership elected at the Nasrec conference, including NEC and the Top Six, was a concoction that sent out the message that the Zuma dragon, while defeated, had not been slain.

The NEC was chock-full of Zuma loyalists, who are also well represented both in Cabinet and in parliamentary committees. This was not a concern for many after the Nasrec conference, with the presumption that Ramaphosa would eventually wield executive authority to drive his political agenda in government. Zuma's loyalists would eventually do Ramaphosa's bidding, the thinking went. Since then, many journalists and commentators have admitted that this reading of the outcome of the Nasrec conference was based more on hope than logic. The Zuma loyalists were able to hold Ramaphosa back, even though he was able to outmanoeuvre them in certain areas.

The Nasrec conference also presented an interesting middle road concerning the composition of the Top Six. Here, Ramaphosa has been flanked by die-hard Zuma allies such as Jessie Duarte and (until his suspension) Ace Magashule. While this raised red flags about the ability of the Top Six to lead the ANC in a difficult moment of realignment, the Top Six also included former Gauteng premier Paul Mashatile and former Zuma ally Gwede Mantashe. The man in the middle is Deputy President David Mabuza, seen as responsible for orchestrating the results at Nasrec by 'betraying' Nkosazana Dlamini-Zuma in her leadership race against Ramaphosa. Had it not been for Mabuza's complex agenda at Nasrec, Dlamini-Zuma would have won the ANC presidency, putting Zuma allies firmly in power.

This type of divided arrangement that is neither here nor there about the direction of the party will not be possible at the next elective conference of the ANC. The party has run out of runway, and it ought to move only in a clear direction. Voters will view another set of compromises as proof that the ANC has stagnated.

It is worth noting that the Nasrec leadership settlement did not come out of deliberate efforts by interest groups to reach a compromise. It came out of a perceived political betrayal. Disgruntled conference delegates nearly contested the results, little realising that the Nasrec results would end up boosting the party at the ballot box in 2019.

It is unlikely that the warring ANC factions will entertain a compromise in terms of leadership to be elected at the next ANC national conference. Further, a false sense of confidence rules in both factions. One faction believes that merely beating the drum of radical economic transformation will exonerate the party from accountability for the large-scale looting during the state capture years. They believe that their crusade against the continued domination of white-owned businesses (the dreaded 'white monopoly capital') provides a moral basis upon which they should be allowed to lead, despite their poor record in addressing structural problems in the economy. For this lot, compromise is a no-go area. They believe their victory in the ANC directly translates into electoral victory in the country.

On the other side of the fence stands a faction that believes it can prevail at the elective conference of the ANC despite the uphill task of reforming the party from within. This requires that groundwork is done at party level, the work they prefer not to do. This is the faction that wants to believe that the moral basis to lead, as seen in the eyes of the broader South African population, should also lie with the ANC, without work being done within the party to realign it. This faction is not known for holding a position in the ANC; it is perpetually in search of a compromise. It is a faction that is not in the business of picking fights on the issues in the ANC. The dominant factions within the ANC declare victory at every turn, because they believe they are in control of the situation.

In this scenario, a political compromise is difficult to imagine, unless the dice fall a certain way, as they did at Nasrec.

At the 2022 conference, the party will have to take a clear stance on whether it is an establishment party that pursues its agenda while being part of the system, or whether it is a revolutionary party that adopts an anti-establishment posture and pursues its agenda by challenging the system. In the last three decades of democracy, the ANC has been able to have it both ways: enjoying an existence as a party that is part of the establishment in which it exercises political power, but at the same time walking away from the establishment by pursuing anti-establishment politics, including openly challenging the judiciary's legitimacy to make decisions that affect the party's policy. In this respect the ANC has blurred the lines between the party and the state, with the party sometimes being used to take an activist anti-establishment position against the judiciary when its judgments reflect negatively on senior party members.

The future of the ANC and the direction of the country until the 2024 elections hinge on the 2022 conference. The message the party sends out will be contained less in the wording of policy documents than in the types of leaders who emerge from the conference. It can no longer dodge key decisions, such as clarity about the country's future economic direction and the fight against corruption.

The giant will soon be standing before its Rubicon.

FOURTEEN
Pretenders to the crown

Could the ANC's next generation of young leaders please step forward?

Amid all the infighting raging in the ruling party it is easy to miss the elephant in the room: a rapidly ageing leadership, with precious few young leaders being groomed to succeed them.

At the time of writing, the average age of the Top Six ANC national office bearers was 63. By the time the ANC holds its next elective conference, in December 2022, the youngest member of the Top Six will be 61 years old – the party's treasurer-general, Paul Mashatile. By then, President Cyril Ramaphosa would have just turned 70. Of course, politicians tend to retire much later in their lives than most other people, but the fact remains that the ANC's top leadership is by no stretch of the imagination made up of young, energetic politicians.

Many other local parties have the same problem, but the situation in the DA and IFP has recently changed. The former is now led by John Steenhuisen (46) and the latter by the 56-year-old Velenkosini Hlabisa. The EFF leadership is mostly young: Julius Malema is 40 years old and his deputy, Floyd Shivambu, is 38.

Ramaphosa will surely be the strongest candidate and the favourite for the top spot at the 2022 elective conference. Tradition dictates that he should walk straight into a second term. Even former president Jacob Zuma was not deposed by his deputy after his first term, in spite of all the controversy his leadership had already created. Zuma successfully pushed back against the deputy president of the party at the time, Kgalema Motlanthe, who challenged him.

However, traditions are no longer all that is relevant in the ANC and Ramaphosa can expect to be challenged.

Let us take a look at possible candidates, at this stage, who could step forward or become increasingly influential in the party's future, starting with the other members of the Top Six.

Had his past not caught up with him, Ace Magashule, suspended secretary-general of the ANC, would surely have been in the mix in 2022.

During research I have carried out in the Free State province, where Magashule's political power base lies, the palpable reach of his power – even to the tiniest local municipality – could not be ignored. Magashule is feared in the Free State for political repercussions that often hit those who challenged his authority. In the explosive book by journalist Pieter-Louis Myburgh, *Gangster State* (2019), Magashule emerges as someone surrounded by a fog of corruption and who built an extensive network during his term as premier of the province. Magashule's tentacles reach far and deep, and for a long time it seemed that he was above the law, above party sanctions. Until he was charged with corruption in relation to the so-called asbestos roof scandal in the Free State.

A private company was grossly overpaid to count houses with asbestos roofs in government-developed townships in the province, with the aim of replacing them. Magashule has been implicated in the tender of R255 million, but the Public Protector found that only R21 million of that amount was actually spent on auditing roofs.[94]

---

94 Modiba, I. 2020. Accused in multimillion Free State asbestos saga to appear in court. SABC News, 11 November 2020. https://www.sabcnews.com/sabc-news/accused-in-multimillion-free-state-asbestos-saga-to-appear-in-court/. Last accessed 14/05/2021.

It was baffling how, in spite of long-standing allegations against him, he survived so long in the party's top structure and how he was able to maintain his influence in the Free State.

Magashule was snubbed by President Thabo Mbeki during his presidency when he refused to appoint him as premier of the Free State. At that stage, Magashule was provincial chairperson of the ANC.

He then focused on consolidating his power in the Free State, growing the support he would need to help orchestrate the eventual removal of Mbeki. When Jacob Zuma was inaugurated as president of South Africa in 2009, he appointed Magashule as premier. Armed with massive popularity and as a flag-bearer against Mbeki, he went to work immediately. He built a complex network that would guarantee him a hold over the Free State, as well as influence over a faction within the party, even after he was deployed to the national office of the ANC as secretary-general.

Given his background, it would have been difficult for the party to survive at the ballot box with Magashule at the helm. His ascent would have spelled an immediate crisis for the principle of rule of law in the country and his election would have been interpreted as an offence to the nation, which would have accelerated the party's electoral decline.

Another interesting figure, and perhaps the most difficult to pin down, is the party's deputy president, David Mabuza.

Should Ramaphosa be incapacitated, Mabuza will take the reins. Once again, according to tradition Mabuza will have to wait for Ramaphosa to complete his second term before he stands up as natural successor. But neither of those scenarios is guaranteed in the current ANC environment.

If Mabuza successfully deposes Ramaphosa in 2022, it would be a historic victory since he would be the first deputy president of the ANC to manage that.

Mabuza is often seen as a political survivor who maintains his position in spite of rumours, allegations and innuendo. The most extensive exposé of his politics was published on 4 August 2018 by *The New York Times*, written by their then local chief correspondent Norimitsu Onishi and Selam Gebrekidan.[95]

They reached the same conclusion as I did, that Mabuza got the deputy presidentship by playing both sides at the ANC elective conference at Nasrec in 2017. He achieved this via his hold on the Mpumalanga province, where he was premier at the time. He has huge experience of grassroots politics and the ability to build large support on that level. It became clear weeks before the conference[96] already that Mabuza was playing both Ramaphosa and his opponent, Nkosazana Dlamini-Zuma, to sneak in his agenda. In a feigned show of unity, he basically picked the president while earning the deputy president position.

However, it will be difficult for Mabuza to repeat his Nasrec move. There is increasing pressure on him to answer to the Integrity Commission of the ANC. He appeared before the commission shortly before he was inaugurated as deputy president after the May 2019 national and provincial elections. He said he wanted his name to be cleared before taking office. However, the commission report did not clear him, even though he insists it did.[97]

---

95 Onishi, N. & Gebrekidan, S. 2018. South Africa vows to end corruption: Are its new leaders part of the problem? *The New York Times*, 4 August 2018. https://www.nytimes.com/2018/08/04/world/africa/south-africa-anc-david-mabuza.html. Last accessed 14/05/2021.
96 Mathekga, R. 2017. Mabuza's clever ploy to control the ANC. News24, 4 December 2017. https://www.news24.com/news24/Columnists/Ralph_Mathekga/mabuzas-clever-ploy-to-control-the-anc-20171204. Last accessed 14/05/2021.
97 Deklerk, A. & Cele, S. 2020. 'We never exonerated David Mabuza' – ANC integrity commission. *TimesLIVE*, 2 August 2020. https://www.timeslive.co.za/sunday-times/news/2020-08-02-we-never-exonerated-david-mabuza-anc-integrity-commission/. Last accessed 14/05/2021.

According to a report by the commission, Mabuza is among 22 ANC leaders who need to explain themselves after allegations of corruption have been made against them. In his case, it is related to his time as Mpumalanga premier, but there are also more recent allegations against him relating to large-scale corruption at Eskom.

His key coordinating role in Cabinet has also irked many, who see it as a mockery of Ramaphosa's advertised 'new dawn' without corruption. The DA complained vehemently when Ramaphosa appointed him to lead the interministerial committee on COVID-19 vaccines,[98] saying Mabuza is prone to corruption and his appointment undermines government's response to the pandemic.

Mabuza is a survivor and he will most likely survive the next elective conference of the ANC as well. However, it is unlikely that he would challenge for the top position, given the current national focus on corruption.

In any case, some of the other provinces, such as KwaZulu-Natal, North West and the Free State, could see Mabuza as someone who betrayed the Zuma grouping. Before 2017, this grouping had strong support in Mabuza's Mpumalanga, Magashule's Free State and Supra Mahumapelo's North West. Both Magashule and Mahumapelo thereafter regrouped against Ramaphosa, openly challenging his leadership. However, this was sans David Mabuza.

With the party as divided as it is, Mabuza could possibly show strong support for a campaign to help Ramaphosa maintain his position, because the president's removal could destabilise his own position.

---

98 AmaShabalala, M. 2021. David Mabuza to lead inter-ministerial committee on vaccines. *TimesLIVE*, 19 January 2021. https://www.timeslive.co.za/politics/2021-01-19-david-mabuza-to-lead-inter-ministerial-committee-on-vaccines/. Last accessed 14/05/2021.

Someone who has supported Ramaphosa throughout is Paul Mashatile, current treasurer-general of the party and Top Six member. Mashatile is very influential in Gauteng, with its large number of voters. He and provincial premier David Makhura tactically aligned themselves with Ramaphosa and, before his election, saw to it that the largest part of the ANC in the province distanced themselves from Zuma.

When asked by journalists about senior leaders of the ANC in Gauteng, I often point out that they are dealing with eloquent and witty people who are also hard to pin down. The ANC government in Gauteng and the provincial structures of the party always take a firm stance on impropriety and corruption, yet they oversee one of the most corrupt provincial administrations in the country.

The Gauteng provincial government has been embroiled in health-related corruption since way back when, and topped it off in 2020 with a new scandal when massive tender corruption involving the purchase of PPE to fight the COVID-19 pandemic came to light. This resulted in the dismissal of health MEC Dr Bandile Masuku.[99]

Makhura himself was briefly embroiled in the scandal after a special tribunal on the issue stated that he had given a list of companies that could benefit from the tender to the province's chief financial officer. Makhura pointed out that his office had supplied the list, and not him, and the tribunal exonerated him of wrongdoing – indeed admitting that it had omitted the words 'Office of' from the report. However, the incident did increase the pressure on

---

99 Retief, C. 2020. Gauteng MEC Dr Bandile Masuku on leave amid Covid-19 corruption allegations. *Daily Maverick*, 30 July 2020. https://www.dailymaverick.co.za/article/2020-07-30-gauteng-health-mec-bandile-masuku-on-leave-amid-covid-19-corruption-allegations/. Last accessed 14/05/2021.

Makhura, especially from certain political groups involved in factionalism, such as the ANC Youth League.[100]

Mashatile served in the provincial government for a long time, which included a short stint as premier after Mbhazima Shilowa resigned in 2008 in protest at Mbeki's removal from office. It will not be easy to sell Mashatile to the nation as a new broom because of the serious problems with service delivery and corruption in the province. Within the party, however, Mashatile has good potential and has the energy to campaign, possibly, for the top job in the party.

He will probably be seen as someone with a large and important constituency (Gauteng), but will not be readily accepted by KwaZulu-Natal because of his stance against Zuma. He should be able to gain support in Limpopo, which is often aligned with Gauteng when it comes to succession decisions in the party, and Ramaphosa's faction in the Eastern Cape will be able to live with Mashatile as a candidate.

No other member of the Top Six should make an impact on leadership change. Mantashe, current national chairperson of the party, is 66 years old and has been in the Top Six for too long. The chances of his leading the party are slim. By next year, his membership of that group will be fifteen years old, having also served as secretary-general for two terms under Zuma.

His record in the Top Six is nearly matched by acting secretary-general Jessie Duarte, who is currently 67. She is in her ninth year as member of the Top Six and has nothing much to offer as a leader in the party.

Outside the Top Six, we do find a couple of interesting personali-

---

[100] Feketha, S. 2021. Makhura cleared of PPE scandal. IOL, 3 February 2021. https://www.iol.co.za/news/politics/makhura-cleared-of-ppe-scandal-5d655a46-b2fe-4a18-84a9-1746df68f132. Last accessed 14/05/2021.

ties who warrant attention. One of them is Ronald Lamola, the 37-year-old Minister of Justice and Correctional Services. Lamola exhibits all the traits of what a young politician ought to be. He is measured, engaging and imaginative. He is one of the young ministers who perform really well – on top of that, in the portfolio that oversees the most critical aspect of the state: the rule of law. Trained as a lawyer, Lamola once cut a lone figure when he protested against Zuma's continued leadership outside a 2016 meeting of the party's NEC in Irene, Pretoria. At that stage he was deputy leader of the ANCYL and he joined a handful of placard-carrying protesters who stuck their necks out outside the meeting venue.

Earlier he had served under Julius Malema in the youth wing, but their divorce had been a rather acrimonious one. After Malema was kicked out of the ANCYL, Lamola substituted for him, which led to the former youth leader trying hard to belittle him.[101] Lamola also urged young voters not to support Malema's EFF.

He does not support factional politics. (He has served in the Mpumalanga government under Mabuza, interestingly, and in 2012 said that the ANCYL would support whoever won at the Mangaung elective conference, where Zuma was re-elected.) He has an independent mind and is not shy to defend ANC policies.

Lamola is more of an activist and one of very few party leaders to have survived the clutches of corruption. He is well-spoken and engaging, and enjoys the support of Ramaphosa, who brought him back to politics after he left it to pursue his law career, appointing him to government.

Someone who could possibly join him in the party's top structures

---

101 Staff Reporter. 2012. 'He's a traitor': Malema lashes out at 'small boy' Lamola. *Mail & Guardian*, 28 November 2012. https://mg.co.za/article/2012-11-28-hes-a-traitor-malema-lashes-out-at-small-boy-lamola/. Last accessed 14/05/2021.

is Stella Ndabeni-Abrahams, one of the rising stars within the ANC. As Minister of Communications and Digital Technologies, she irked the nation during the COVID-19 lockdown when pictures were posted on social media showing her violating lockdown rules. She was reprimanded by Ramaphosa.

More importantly, though, her husband, Thato, has been implicated in possible tender irregularities in a government agency overseen by Ndabeni-Abrahams. His name is mentioned in a report of the Universal Service and Access Agency (Usaasa) on irregularities and maladministration within the organisation from April 2009 to the end of September 2011.[102]

Ndabeni, 43, is politically active and, although sophisticated, she remains accessible. She has also not aligned herself with the ANC Women's League, which insisted on supporting Zuma, but rather aligned herself with Ramaphosa. She is a possible candidate for the top leadership in the ANC.

Another key person to watch is KwaZulu-Natal's premier, Sihle Zikalala (47). He is a former Zuma ally who has carefully crafted a political living space for himself between Zuma and Ramaphosa. He uses his premiership to speak out on corruption while not ruffling feathers within the party in the province about the issue. Zikalala is managing to survive in the most volatile provincial structure of the ANC, where Zuma is still very influential.

He cooperates with Ramaphosa and amplifies the president's agenda in his provincial government, while not overstepping certain boundaries so that he can survive in a Ramaphosa-hostile

---

[102] Mdluli, A. 2020. Stella Ndabeni's husband implicated in Usaasa theft. IOL, 11 September 2020. https://www.iol.co.za/news/politics/stella-ndabenis-husband-implicated-in-usaasa-theft-07749d53-e5e7-4c0a-a462-763ea96d-cfc3. Last accessed 14/05/2021.

province. At the next elective conference Zikalala will be 49, making him a strong future candidate for the Top Six leadership of the party.

Many other young party leaders had all their leadership prospects wiped out by the blight of corruption, for example the minister of many Zuma portfolios, Malusi Gigaba. Other leaders have fallen into the quagmire of party factions. Fikile Mbalula is on this list, having flip-flopped between factions to the point where nobody knows where he stands any more.

Zizi Kodwa, Deputy Minister of State Security and former spokesperson for the party, is another who comes to mind. Kodwa has been cleared by the ANC's Integrity Commission after his name came up during testimony before the Zondo Commission. According to the party commission's report, he admitted to receiving R375 000 from EOH Holdings, but stated that he had been given financial assistance by the company.[103]

If you really have to, you can scrape the bottom of the ANC barrel and come up with Lindiwe Sisulu's name as an influential personality to keep in mind. She has attempted to become a candidate for the ANC presidency before, when Ramaphosa campaigned towards the 2017 Nasrec elective conference. But Lindiwe Sisulu has just about only her strong struggle credentials to fall back on, as well as her heritage as member of an important and influential political family. She has no real constituents in the ANC, nor in the country. Neither has she been a successful minister in any department she has led – from housing to intelligence to defence.

When it comes to grooming leaders to take over the party, the

---

103 Ntshidi, E. 2021. Zizi Kodwa welcomes ANC's report clearing him of state capture wrongdoing. Eyewitness News, 31 January 2021. https://ewn.co.za/2021/01/31/zizi-kodwa-welcomes-anc-s-report-clearing-him-of-state-capture-wrongdoing. Last accessed 14/05/2021.

ANC is falling short. Its top leaders are ageing. Party elders are regularly called upon to lead because there is a vacuum below them – the young people in the party lack capacity to lead. The ANC's political school has also not produced leaders with any pedigree to lead in a modern, complex society. This is a concern that the party should address if it intends to survive.

FIFTEEN
Ramaphosa's legacy

President Cyril Ramaphosa enjoys the rare distinction of being loved more by a large number of voters outside his party than by a significant section of his party. This, of course, is in large part due to the deep divisions in the ANC – in many respects, it currently houses two parties in one.

For the ANC's so-called RET faction – which once marched in lockstep behind former president Jacob Zuma – Ramaphosa is enemy number one. The one who turned off the tap of government largesse. The one who insists that government institutions and SOEs are not the ANC's milch cow. Ramaphosa's leadership has hit many of his rent-seeking comrades where it hurts most: their wallets.

The ill-will directed at Ramaphosa from this faction should not be underestimated. It manifested itself publicly in the desperate attempt by Ace Magashule to 'suspend' Ramaphosa after he himself had been suspended as secretary-general of the party. With that, any pretence of 'party unity' since Nasrec 2017 dissipated once and for all – not that too many people were buying it to begin with.

It is fairly hard to imagine a DA voter rooting for the heir to the Zupta faction in this fight. Rather, most are holding thumbs that Ramaphosa keeps the RET grouping at bay and retains control over the ANC, although they themselves would never consider voting for the party he leads.

The election results in Gauteng in 2019 even point to the existence of an interesting subset of voters with a seemingly special affinity for the president. On the ballot for the National Assembly, the ANC received 53,2 per cent of the votes cast in Gauteng. But in voting for the provincial legislature, it scraped home with 50,19 per cent. One plausible explanation for the disparity of 3 percentage points is Ramaphosa's popularity among the middle class in Gauteng. Where he was the face of the party (the national ballot), they chose the ANC; where he was not, they chose one of the opposition parties.

Despite the challenges he has faced in reforming his party, Ramaphosa has made strides in tackling corruption at state level. He has championed the return of principles such as accountability and integrity in government. In these endeavours, he has not always met with unqualified success, but at least a solid foundation has been built after the state capture years laid waste to our government institutions. For South Africa to leave this era behind, the leader who comes after Ramaphosa – whenever that may be – will have to build on this legacy. Ramaphosa himself may be judged on the leadership pipeline he leaves behind.

In my previous book, I argued that the president's style of leadership is better understood in the context of the mass-based United Democratic Front (UDF), where Ramaphosa cut his teeth as a leader. The principles instilled in him there have seen him favouring an approach of wider, lateral consultation as opposed to the hierarchical approach inherent in the system of democratic centralism preached by the ANC. Ramaphosa has raised the expectations of what South Africans may demand of their leaders, sparking hope that his legacy will outlive his own tenure, however long it may last.

Ramaphosa could very well gain a second term and continue as president of the country after the next national and provincial elections in 2024, either through a narrow absolute majority in the National Assembly or as the leader of a coalition government if the

ANC dips below 50 per cent. That would mean that his leadership style and his political agenda survive until the 2029 elections.

Still, we must consider what type of leader might emerge from Ramaphosa's shadow when he departs. Which leadership strategies would he have left behind, and how will they influence the thinking about leadership in the country going forward?

One of Ramaphosa's primary leadership traits is that he leans towards collective decision-making. For a businessman leading South Africa, Ramaphosa has been reserved in his approach. He does not often use the word 'I'. He prefers the word 'we' to the point of discomfort from the business community, which expects 'one of their own' to take charge of the political and economic crises in the country and accept individual responsibility. In this regard, Ramaphosa has been a disappointment to those who expected a Donald Trump-like style of rapid and impulsive decision-making to deal with immediate concerns.

Ramaphosa's concept of 'we', however, differs from what the ANC means when it uses the word. When the ANC says 'we' in the context of democratic centralism, the party is not talking about consultation. Ramaphosa, however, has been more consultative in his decision-making. He has notably used wider forums such as independent panels of inquiry to assist him in making key decisions, including appointing the National Director of Public Prosecutions, Advocate Shamila Batohi. This is not only because he was such a democrat that he decided to consult widely outside ANC political circles, but also because he had to avoid the compromised political channels in the ANC that would taint his agenda. Ramaphosa has used a similar strategy of appointing independent panels, sometimes led by judges, to offer recommendations about key decisions in government.

Despite conditions that conspired towards wider consultation on important decisions, the experience as far as South Africans are concerned is that of a system in which the power to make key decisions is not concentrated in the hands of a few politicians. South Africans would also expect in the future that important decisions are made through consultative processes that involve diverse stakeholders in society, and not only a few politicians wielding executive prerogative. Because he did not enjoy total control in the ANC, Ramaphosa found himself having to go out of his way to use independent panels to help him arrive at decisions that would have been challenged had he reached them by exercising his executive authority.

Decision-making through credible panels of inquiry is a more apt approach when power is beginning to be dispersed from the centre. Ramaphosa took the reins of the ANC and the country at precisely such a time. Ramaphosa's approach is pragmatic, and it has also demonstrated that not all key decisions in the state should effectively be left to the sole prerogative of politicians. Ramaphosa's tendency to undertake elaborate consultative processes when making key decisions can be frustrating to those who demand immediate action from the president.

An alternative approach to leadership in this regard would be a strong executive leader, who makes decisions quickly and owns them. With government decisions increasingly being challenged in court, such a leader could face some hurdles in an increasingly litigious society. Ramaphosa's approach takes longer to deliver results because panels have to meet and investigate, and ultimately issue a report with recommendations that Ramaphosa has been consistent in implementing. Under Zuma's leadership, South Africans were not consulted on key decisions. This even resulted in a complaint by some members of the judiciary that too many key decisions, including the appointment of the National Director of Public Prosecutions, were too highly concentrated in the executive.

Various NPA appointments that Zuma made were later declared by the courts to be constitutionally unjustifiable. This has to do with the process followed and the nature of the individual appointed to the position. Zuma's appointment of Menzi Simelane as NPA boss was overturned on judicial review because Simelane was not fit for the job. The same fate befell Advocate Shaun Abrahams, another Zuma appointee. There was also the troubled appointment and sudden dismissal of Mxolisi Nxasana as head of the NPA. Ramaphosa remedied this situation by involving independent panels to assist him in removing unjustifiable appointments at the NPA. This has seen the removal of prosecutors Nomgcobo Jiba and Lawrence Mrwebi.

Should South Africans dream of a more forceful leader than Ramaphosa? The country is still in its early stages of experimenting with political leadership under democracy, and the journey will be tumultuous. The search for a post-Ramaphosa leader should begin by identifying the type of leadership style that Ramaphosa has showcased. Often accused of being too much of a consensus seeker, Ramaphosa has placed South Africa's politics on a path that would require consultative leaders who spread the responsibility to govern across various institutions and do not concentrate power in a few hands. Ramaphosa's practical approach to decision-making has put him on a collision course with the ANC's principle of democratic centralism, which effectively entails domination by senior members of the party while the rank and file remains disciplined and allows senior leaders to lead.

Given our country's history – both before and after the dawn of democracy – South Africans should harbour a deep distrust of leaders who wield absolute executive power. I find the consultative approach much more attractive, even if it leads to some delays in decision-making. The crisis of leadership experienced by South

Africa under the ANC dictates that the country rethink its expectations regarding leadership. While it may be enticing for some to imagine a strong leader with integrity who is able to ride roughshod over objections and divisions, this leadership style brings more risk into the political system. A strong, reliable leader can indeed provide an immediate solution to a country that has been indecisive about policy direction. However, it is only a matter of time until an unscrupulous strong leader comes along and abuses the same power given to the benign strong leader.

The idea that a benign dictator needs to emerge within the ANC to solve South Africa's political and economic problems is quite risky to entertain. Within the ANC, choices are extremely limited when it comes to the type of leadership that may emerge after Ramaphosa. The best-case scenario in terms of the country experiencing a consultative presidency after Ramaphosa would be if one of his allies takes over the party. The risk to the country is if an executive-minded, majoritarian leader emerges from the RET faction to take over from Ramaphosa – and the absolute worst-case scenario is if this happens as early as the elective conference in December 2022. I do not believe this scenario is highly likely, but it would have huge ramifications for both party and country. The era of 'might makes right' would return. Democratic centralism would once again rear its head in institutions of the state.

This scenario would see the ANC at a high risk of losing its absolute majority in the 2024 elections and consequently governing through a coalition or, at the very least, with a significantly reduced majority. If this happens, the governing principle of democratic centralism could create a crisis of legitimacy in decision-making. With a reduced majority, the ANC would need a measured leader who understands that the party's political mandate has been dented by the return of the faction intimately associated with the corruption of the state capture years. In this situation, consultation would be necessary to legitimise decisions. The decisions of this putative post-Ramaphosa administration would run the risk of being blocked in the courts – as happened countless times during the Zuma years – or of being stymied through other forms of disruption, such as public protest and mass action.

As mentioned, I do not believe that the above scenario is very likely, but it would be unwise to discount it. History has shown us that the ANC can unseat a president.

Moving away from the worst-case scenario, our best hope is that the principles of consultative leadership and clean governance established by Ramaphosa are cemented and set the standard for future leaders. If these principles prevail, it will not matter whether Ramaphosa is the president.

However, these principles are under threat from more than just a powerful faction within the ANC. At this moment in history, the world seems increasingly to be turning towards executive-minded populist leaders who vow to confront and upend the system. This brings me to the EFF's leadership style, and how that would fit in a South Africa that has endured executive domination under the guise of the pursuit of a transformation project. While the EFF is highly unlikely to win power itself, it would have a good chance of governing alongside the ANC if the ruling party falls below 50 per cent and has to govern through a coalition.

The EFF's approach to leadership follows the contours of the ANC's concept of democratic centralism – a party dominated by leaders at the top who make key decisions on behalf of the rank and file of the party. The EFF believes in majoritarianism, under which consensus is not a basis for justifying decisions. Consensus is regarded as unnecessary when a strong majority exists. The challenge with the EFF is that its policy trajectory and approach to leadership do not take into consideration the objective conditions of political fragmentation and dispersion of power from the centre. What this means is that South African politics is naturally shifting towards consensus-driven politics, as majoritarian politics has created deadlocks and abuse of power. The EFF believes in strong executive leadership, which may spook the middle class, who are worried about the abuse of power under majoritarian politics. The EFF unfortunately does not offer an alternative to the ANC when it comes to leadership style, and the party would find it difficult to navigate competing interests if it were to come to power.

This, then, leaves the DA as a place where consensus leadership could be cherished. The DA is known for demanding accountability from the ANC, and the party has waged successful court challenges relating to some of the executive decisions that have been made under the ANC. The DA has also noted that lack of consensus is, indeed, a major blockage in South Africa's policy pipeline. However, the party has taken a direction that raises questions about whether it can provide a leadership alternative any longer. It has seemingly shifted away from the middle ground, and started to become increasingly focused on fighting identity politics wars. This makes it difficult for it to build a majority-driven opposition party that opposes from the centre, and not from the fringes of identity politics. Even if the DA says it believes in consensus leadership, its recent turn in terms of opposition style is leading the party away from the centre, where consensus is possible.

In conclusion, what comes after Ramaphosa would depend on how South Africans reflect on Ramaphosa's leadership. South Africa is experiencing an irreversible political fragmentation and the search for the grand majority as a basis for political action is a futile exercise. In this environment of fragmentation, leaders should appreciate the need to consult widely on key decisions to ensure that decisions retain legitimacy to be implemented. A strong executive leader will find it difficult to lead a fragmented society and will be prone to endless disruptions. The consensus-driven leadership style favoured by Ramaphosa is the way forward.

The ANC would do well to abandon the concept of democratic centralism entirely. It limits the party's ability to bring forth leaders who will attract voters in a fragmented society. The party has entered an era in which it will have to work much harder to earn its votes. We have lost the political innocence that has sustained the ANC's domination for the past three decades of democracy.

As to who or what comes after Ramaphosa, that should be dictated by the way in which the nation's consciousness about leadership is evolving. At this point, South Africans have experienced noticeable returns when political leadership is consultative and functions by engaging instead of excluding. This is a message that the nation ought to carry forward as it assesses leaders in the future. South Africa needs leaders who will not concentrate power in their own hands, and such leaders are generally in short supply across the world. One hopes, however, that leaders will read the atmosphere correctly and understand that the current fragmentation can be dealt with through consensus politics instead of artificial cosmetic unity that ultimately subverts the voice of the people.

The tracks for better leadership have been laid. What remains is the matter of whether we follow them, or take a detour.

SIXTEEN
South Africa's giant slayers

A few years ago, I was invited to take part in a brown-bag lunch discussion organised by the South African chapter of the global NGO Oxfam. These debates are always illuminating because the organisation brings in its local community partners, who are not afraid to challenge speakers when their theoretical concepts do not match up with practical realities on ground level.

In this particular discussion, I was asked to talk about how our country's Constitution relates to the concept of social justice. As is customary, the meeting included activists from community-based organisations across South Africa. I knew that they would not be framing their questions diplomatically but through the lens of their own grassroots experiences.

I was holding forth about how South Africa's Constitution is among the most progressive in the world because it also allows for activism when I was challenged by one of the participants. They retorted that, in their experience, the Constitution was a useful tool in the hands of a few, particularly white-dominated civil rights groups such as AfriForum and the trade union Solidarity. Of course, it is an exaggeration that the Constitution has only been utilised by those groups. It is, however, concerning that a part of society believes that the Constitution is useful only to those who already have power.

There is no doubt that the powerful will use all available institutions to access remedies in a society. The poor, on the other hand, depend on the government and non-governmental organisations to access constitutional remedies. The noose tightens for the poor when government is reluctant to help them access those remedies. When only those with resources can access constitutional remedies, it is not a well-ordered society. If the poor and vulnerable become convinced that democratic principles and remedies are not available to them, they will disengage and disrupt the system.

I still maintain that our Constitution offers much to the poor and vulnerable, but that they should be aided and encouraged to find their voice and, where necessary, approach the courts. In this, ironically, NGOs can play a leading role. The fact that the current power balance does not readily allow the poor and the vulnerable to access certain remedies does not mean they should disengage with the system.

Towards the end of the meeting, two participants approached me and told me they wanted to discuss my ideas about the Constitution and social justice in greater detail. From there, I met the two gentlemen over coffee where we discussed the various constitutional implications of policy activism and so forth. The two also mentioned that they were trying to find a way to reform South Africa's electoral system using nothing but the courts. Their public interest organisation, the New Nation Movement – at that stage, an obscure outfit that I had never heard of – was pursuing court litigation to nullify electoral law because it did not allow for independent candidates to stand in general elections.

When the two first outlined their idea of court action, I thought I was listening to Don Quixote prior to his first tilt at the windmill. I did not see how this unknown group could bring about a seismic shift in the South African political landscape. Firstly, it soon became apparent that they did not have deep pockets. Secondly, they were not from one of the usual suspects that had a track record on policy litigation in South Africa. I was impressed with their enthusiasm for people power, and thought their approach was raising some interesting research questions but had little chance of practical success.

Nonetheless, I found our discussions illuminating. As a political analyst, one can sometimes get trapped in an ivory tower, but these activists were giving me insight into the innovative thinking going on at ground level in our country – ideas that are often glossed over without getting a proper airing. They were about to change that.

They state on their website that their organisation, the New Nation Movement, is not a political party, it is a 'network of like-minded South Africans'.[104] When I asked them whether there was anything in it for them, they emphatically stated they want to support democracy by supporting independent candidates.

After three years of staying in touch with them since the Oxfam discussion, the two won a Constitutional Court victory in 2020, declaring the current electoral law in the country unconstitutional because it does not allow independent candidates to stand for provincial and national elections. When the news of the court victory broke in June 2020, journalists in South Africa scrambled, trying to make sense of how such a seemingly insignificant organisation whose members had such unassuming personalities had been able to win such a significant court victory.

It was like David slaying Goliath – or, in this case, a giant.

The fact that the face of the poor and the vulnerable could secure a court victory that would trigger a long journey of electoral reform in South Africa is indicative of the latent potential in our country. There is enormous upside if we can get our democracy firing on all cylinders.

---

104 New Nation Movement. https://newnation.org.za/.

In South Africa, ordinary people without resources can approach the court and spark a policy reform from below. The ANC government had no intention to undertake electoral reform in line with how our society has evolved. If the dominant political leaders are unwilling to effect policy changes, the court can take the role of setting the country on a path of policy reform at the behest of only one or two daring individuals.

One of the greatest impediments to the consolidation of South Africa's democracy is that we sometimes tend only to look to powerful institutions and hope that they will implement change from the top down. The *New Nation* case triggered electoral reform from below. Of course, a powerful institution – in this case, the Constitutional Court – was also involved, but it was ordinary South Africans who got the ball rolling. This shows how South Africa's institutions are aligned to complement each other. If policy output is lacking from the political leaders, members of civil society can ask the courts to place the country on a reform path.

When I look at how South Africa has advanced despite poor leadership from the ANC, it becomes clear that political leadership is not only available through a political party. Furthermore, where there is deficit in terms of political leadership, citizens can approach multiple levels of lateral leadership dispersed across state institutions. South Africa has a decentralised bureaucratic system, including a distinctly decentralised anti-corruption apparatus. For example, a politically connected person serving in government might be investigated for corruption by multiple government agencies, some even working independently. The advantage of the decentralised system is that, even if there are political blockages elsewhere, the system should still be able to function in general.

If one attempts to block the investigation by discouraging the police from investigating because they are controlled by the executive, a constitutional institution such as the office of the Public Protector or the Auditor-General may undertake an independent inquiry into the same matter. With multiple points of accountability in a complex system, South Africa's bureaucratic alignment – including the principle of separation of powers – functions to advance reforms that the political leadership fails to pursue. Democratic institutions should not rely excessively on incumbents to function – they should be based on shared principles and practices that keep them functioning irrespective of the whims of the office bearers.

The main challenge that South Africa has encountered is its political leadership, specifically that of the ANC. With the ANC losing legitimacy, an opportunity exists for South Africans to begin to reimagine some of the projects that are vital to the nation but have been sullied by the ANC approach. For nearly three decades, the ANC has appropriated the transformation project in South Africa, abusing it to further its own ends and that of its allies, rather than bringing about meaningful change in the broader society.

Fragmentation means that South Africans can now begin to imagine how to transform the country in line with the principles of constitutional supremacy. This will require creativity in terms of policy proposals. Fragmentation could also lead to realignments in terms of political identities. A fragmented and weakened ANC holds some definite advantages for the country as a whole. The unravelling provides new opportunities to reground transformation and a host of other policies. A system dominated by a single political party can make it difficult for the broader population to get a word in edgeways, and leaves all policy in the hands of Plato's all-knowing philosopher kings.

South Africa's vibrant NGO sector played a vital role during the state capture years: holding the central government to account while Parliament was missing in action; challenging irrational decisions by the state in court; and plugging the gaps where service delivery by government institutions fell woefully short.

South Africa's courts have also held up admirably so far. Of all three branches of government – the executive, the legislative and the judiciary – they have done the most to uphold the country's institutional integrity. The judiciary has not been shy in making difficult decisions, at times going against the wishes of the ANC-led government.

Parliament, on the other hand, has been a toothless watchdog, toeing the party line instead of exercising its constitutionally mandated oversight on the executive.

Even when the ANC wields its majority in pushing controversial policies – such as the expropriation of land without compensation – the courts still have a say in refining these measures when legal challenges are launched. In the case of expropriation without compensation, it will take more than a single amendment to weaken the right to private property envisioned in the Constitution significantly. South Africa's Constitution is complex, and its spirit cannot be altered by a couple of amendments. This places the judiciary on a permanent collision course with the executive, however. While the judiciary has played an admirable role in safeguarding the integrity of some of the institutions, it is undesirable for courts to remain the only avenue through which policy engagement is possible.

If the court is constantly engaged in policy litigation, it becomes drawn into daily policy dialogue, something that democratic societies should avoid. Already, the courts are facing criticism that they meddle in political matters when they review policy brought before them. The battle that brings the greater risk to South Africa's democracy is political attacks on the judiciary, or on decisions by its judges. Nonetheless, the judiciary is still regarded as a credible institution by most South Africans and, despite frequent accusations from aggrieved politicians, no hard evidence of any judicial political bias has emerged.

Despite the complaints of the NGOs at the Oxfam discussion, NGOs have had some major successes in approaching the courts to help marginalised citizens – especially concerning policy changes in health and education. South Africa undertook the world's largest anti-HIV programme because of court action launched by the Treatment Action Campaign (TAC). Equal Education, another NGO, has been effective in pushing policy reforms in education through the courts. There have been numerous cases since the presidency of Thabo Mbeki showing that political power to achieve policy goals is dispersed across institutions.

The crisis of legitimacy experienced by the ANC has pushed South Africa towards a multipronged leadership approach, where key decisions in societies are influenced by multiple stakeholders, some of whom operate outside the political realm. This implies, also, that leadership in our society is dispersing from the political centre to multiple centres.

The shift towards multistakeholder involvement in decision-making was born out of the crisis and conflict of the state capture years. But once established, it becomes entrenched, even when the immediate crisis has passed.

The fightback staged by some ANC members against the Constitution and the judiciary lacks moral standing and is not sustainable. I do not see South Africa going into reverse gear to the point at which there are deep doubts about the Constitution and the rule of law. I regard these as some of the irreversible gains of democracy. South Africans are ready to demand more from their political leadership.

Political fragmentation is also experienced in the opposition camp, where consolidation by the major opposition parties is becoming more and more unlikely. The DA and the EFF each occupy separate and distinct niches. The EFF enjoyed some grudging respect during the state capture years because it was a countervailing force to power. Even its critics admit that it gives a voice to the poor and vulnerable. The DA is respected for its record of clean and efficient government at local and provincial level, even as its policy on race threatens to cloud the party's future.

All in all, South Africa is shifting towards a more competitive political system. The backlash in terms of disengagement with the political processes resulting from the collapse of service delivery, for example, has not been significant. South Africans remain largely engaged with the system. As the system evolves, people find new ways of securing some returns from it. When the poor and vulnerable realise that they can get a quicker response from government through litigation than through service delivery protests, the system will turn upside down. Vulnerable communities are already starting to talk the language of court action.

Is South Africa a failed state? My answer is no. However, the country is increasingly accumulating some of the characteristics of a failed state, as basic service delivery collapses and citizens become accustomed to living under those conditions. But South Africa's network of state institutions, including government, is aligned in such a way that the country will not be brought down by poor political leadership.

South Africa has to reconstitute the centre of its politics to ensure that it does not become a bargain democracy, where the strong dominate the weak. The country needs to survive under the new permanent state of weaker and dispersed political leadership. This is a difficult task, as it may lead to unguided and unsanctioned bargaining in a democracy, as I will explain in the final chapter. Democracy cannot be sustained without any attempt to constitute the political centre, guided by the need to unite the nation. Let there be varying ideas about how to achieve that; the idea, however, should not die, or a democracy becomes a system where interest groups define the national agenda as they compete for state influence. My biggest fear is a possible right-wing and nationalistic turn, which could sneak in under the guise of self-determination and further democratisation.

SEVENTEEN
A strange new world

Over the past 70-odd years, South Africans have known only two political dispensations: total control by the National Party from 1948 to 1994 and total control by the ANC from 1994 onwards.

For a country so used to hegemonic rule by a single party, it will be a strange new world indeed if the ANC loses its grip on absolute power in 2024 or 2029.

If the predictions in this book hold true, no political party will, in the medium term, be able to command political hegemony in the way the ANC did in the past three decades of democracy – or, for that matter, the apartheid government in the years before that. South Africa's politics is evolving from below – that is, without being led by a distinct group from above – and this poses a serious threat to the idea of political hegemony as a source of legitimacy in justifying political projects in society.

The Italian philosopher Antonio Gramsci's work on hegemony and how it relates to the democratic bureaucratic state is useful in understanding what will replace it in South African politics. With the ANC's political hegemony declining rapidly towards the end of the third decade of democracy, a critical question becomes how the party would seek to dominate society henceforth. Its appetite to control society and further experiment with its transformation project will not necessarily dissipate with the party's dwindling support and declining domination in society. Following Gramsci's definition, hegemony entails domination by a group throughout society.[105] The source of legitimacy for domination may be historical. In the case of the ANC's political hegemony, the source is the historical prestige of leading the liberation movement. This has allowed the party to shape the trajectory of institutions in a democratic South Africa.

With the ANC losing legitimacy to govern and no longer able to dominate society through its political project, the party will most likely resort to other forms of domination to restore itself to its past position of total control. By the look of things, the ANC's response to continue to dominate a fragmented society is to resort to what Gramsci characterises as 'direct domination or command exercised through the State and judicial government'.[106] The most obvious character of liberation parties is that they find it difficult to survive in a fragmented society where the idea of national questions, as defined at the political centre, becomes less and less relevant in defining agendas across the country. In trying to bring back the glory days of hegemony, the ANC has shown that the party is willing to reconstitute state institutions, including the democratic bureaucracy to allow the party to continue to dominate society.

The sentiment is broadly expressed in the party's growing willingness to assert itself by consolidating power by way of restructuring state institutions. For example, the mooted establishment of district development councils aimed at consolidating and coordinating service delivery across municipalities extends the party's hold in municipalities, despite the growing trend showing that the party is rapidly losing voter support in those municipalities. Because the

---

105 Gramsci, A. 1971. *Selection from Prison Notebooks*. London: Lawrence and Wishart.
106 Ibid., p. 12.

party has squandered its political hegemony, it seeks to restructure state institutions to extend its hold on the country and counteract its declining political power. The ANC justifies this manoeuvre by pointing to the 'urgency' of pursuing a development agenda that is supposed to rise above political squabbles. Essentially, this is a way to create a development hegemony, which is a useful diversion from addressing deep political questions. The greater risk to democracy in South Africa is therefore a quasi-dictatorship under the guise of a developmental state.

Unfortunately, the opposition parties offer little reprieve to push back against a shift towards this 'developmental dictatorship' by the ANC. When it comes to how policy options are framed, the EFF is no different from the hardline, centralised developmental dictatorship modelled by some in the ANC and with historical roots in the party's liberation politics. The EFF has no interest in searching for consensus-driven policy options with a win-win appeal to the broader nation. The EFF is essentially interested in pursuing policies that also have an element of justice as part of their implementation. For example, the land reform policy advocated by the EFF, and subsequently processed into law by Parliament, does not worry about those who stand to lose land, as it is expropriated for the benefits of the historically disadvantaged. The policy only concerns itself with justice and restoration, and does not seek consensus among interested parties about how to resolve this historical problem. Because the law stands to benefit the majority, it is regarded as justifiable. The EFF's approach is in line with the principle of developmental dictatorship and offers no alternative to the ANC in this regard.

The DA's recent shift in policy orientation also raises questions about whether it can pursue unifying progressive politics for reconstituting the political centre that has been vandalised and abandoned by the ANC. In his book *Future Tense*,[107] former DA leader Tony Leon offers an intimate analysis of what happened in the DA that led to the sudden resignation of Mmusi Maimane in October 2019. According to Leon, Maimane led the DA poorly on the race issue, culminating in electoral loss by the party in the 2019 provincial and national elections.

Quite interesting about this intimate observation of what happened in the DA under Maimane is Leon's take on the DA's attempt to form coalition governments in hung metros after the 2016 municipal elections. I share Leon's sentiments that the experience has been horrendous for the DA, with the party being stuck with mayors whose quest to form and sustain DA-led coalitions raised questions about what the DA brand stood for. The coalition experience exposed how the DA's attempt to grow its black constituency challenged the party's broader position on some fundamental issues, including the mere idea of the party entering coalitions with parties such as the EFF, whose leaders' good governance and political integrity records leave much to be desired. The DA was struggling with genuine issues in this regard, however – how should the party embrace its role in constructing a different type of politics based on values shared by South Africans? The poor electoral performance in the 2019 elections resulted in a leadership and policy orientation shift that would raise questions about the DA's ability to construct an alternative, consensus-driven politics.

Indeed, Maimane's leadership tenure in the DA had been tumultuous, but what is worrying is the misdiagnosis that the DA's failure to walk away from the race issue was responsible for the electoral

---

107 Leon, T. 2021. *Future Tense: Reflections on My Troubled Land*. Cape Town: Jonathan Ball Publishers.

stagnation beginning to show in the 2019 elections. The problem here is that being diametrically opposed to the ANC on race is mistaken to imply being a desirable alternative to the party. The DA has become diametrically opposed to the ideals of the ANC when it comes to transformation, and this is making the party less appealing for those who favour centre politics but have been abandoned by the ANC.

Is there a space for centre politics in South Africa? The answer is yes, despite the ANC's efforts to appropriate centre politics in the past three decades of democracy. At this point, the DA has no transformation project, except for arguing for economic growth. This is not a challenge for the DA alone, but also for the broader proponents of the liberal project in post-apartheid South Africa.

In his seminal book *Reconstructing South African Liberalism* (1986), Charles Simkins argued that, for South Africa to be able to sustain a liberal-democratic project, there is a need to reconstruct South Africa's liberalism to ensure that it also acknowledges the burden of past injustices in its attempts to build a prosperous future for all. According to Simkins, standard liberalism, which presumes that everyone can fend for themselves, will not be optimal for South Africa due to the continued impact of past injustices. The ANC government implemented policies aimed to ensure that those who have been previously disadvantaged do not suffer further impediments in the future.

The problem is that the ANC implemented its transformation in an illiberal way, often unjustifiably trampling upon some of the rights enshrined in the Constitution. Simkins' basic argument is that transformation policies can indeed be implemented within a liberal constitutional framework. The ANC has fallen short in this regard, having leaned more towards an illiberal approach in policy implementation. In some sense, the problem is not too complicated when one takes a second look. Let us consider, for example, what it would take to reformulate some of the liberal principles to ensure that they fit the circumstances in South Africa.

Affirmative action and black economic empowerment are among some of the ANC's controversial policies, whose implementation has resulted in concerns being raised – also by the DA – about the party's commitment to the Constitution and the liberal principle that requires all to be treated equally. It can be shown that, in most instances, the ANC did indeed abuse those policy levers in various forms, including corruption during the process of implementation. However, that the ANC could not function properly within a liberal framework does not mean that the idea of constructing a transformation agenda in a liberal constitutional framework is doomed from the beginning. This is a fallacy that shows how South Africa's policy imagination is still being held hostage by the ANC. Rejecting transformation merely because the ANC could not implement it successfully shows that parties such as the DA are essentially set on either rejecting or approving ANC ideas, instead of trying to find a way to rescue certain projects from the ANC.

The DA has decided not to venture into rethinking how progressive centre politics can be rebuilt. Rather, the party has decided to abandon the idea of race as a criterion in public policy. This has also removed transformation from the table for the DA.

The past decade of the ANC's political hegemony is closing in, with the dispersion of political power from the national sphere to the regions. Political fragmentation in the country has also intensified in this decade, and the big three political parties in the country (the EFF, the DA and the ANC) are unsettled in a shifting political landscape. The DA is in survival mode, while the EFF is only looking to consolidate its electoral position as the third-most dominant party in the country. The DA is shifting towards identity politics. It offers a version of liberalism that is too pure and lacks the modification it needs to address the historical conditions encountered in South Africa. The classical version of liberalism that ignores the continued impact of race on access to opportunities would certainly run into legitimacy problems in a similar way that an illiberal approach to policy implementation, relying solely on majoritarianism, would.

It could be a global phenomenon that centre politics, based on national identities and shared unifying agendas, are declining and giving way to identity politics as a new way of challenging the centre that is struggling with legitimacy. This means that the political fragmentation being observed is inevitable, and not necessarily tragic. Fragmentation is, in this regard, a condition for social and political realignment. Like most liberal-oriented Western democracies, including the USA, political fragmentation is giving rise to the emergence of identity politics, resulting in tremors for liberal democracies whose legitimacy had for years been anchored in its centre politics with generally accepted unifying messages.

What has been witnessed in some Western democracies in recent years is the rise of identity politics – and, in some areas, different permutations of nationalism. This brings forth an interesting conversation I have had with political scientist Francis Fukuyama when he came to launch his book *Identity* (2018) in Sandton. Fukuyama has written fascinating works including *The End of History and the Last Man*. The *Identity* book launch was a rare opportunity to quiz a man who is always bold in his projections about some of the major shifts in our society.

My question to Fukuyama had to do with identity politics, the title of his book. I wanted to know whether the rapid emergence of identity politics was a threat to liberalism and its claim to be the most functional system for mediating relations in a political community. I was also curious about how political fragmentation and the resurgence of identity politics could change the course of liberal institutions, including constitutions, setting them on a path of recognition of those identities. If so, then how much was left of liberalism?

There are no conclusive answers to these questions. South Africa's political evolution is also beginning to raise these questions, the same ones that trouble countries that are considered advanced liberal democracies, such as the USA. The battle between identity politics and liberalism will dominate most societies in the medium term, and the results of these struggles will have long-lasting effects on liberal institutions and how they relate to citizens in democracies.

According to Fukuyama, some of the demands for recognition that groups make are difficult to meet, and they will stretch liberal democracies. South Africa's political fragmentation is showing the trend of nationalism and identity politics emerging as points of political mobilisation. For liberal democracies to survive the surge of identity politics, Fukuyama argued that they should offer universal recognition of identities. If the system at the centre does not recognise the way in which groups seek to be recognised in political society, groups will challenge the legitimacy of the system by bargaining outside the system – often, by disrupting the system.

Identity politics usually gains attention from the system by disrupting it. This has become the mode of engagement in South Africa as, increasingly, neither the centre nor the system are seen as representing the plight of marginalised groups.

The level of inequality in South Africa requires us to tackle the problem through a nationally shared agenda that unifies the nation. So the need to rebuild centre politics is necessary for the long-term stability of the country. Development disparities across regions are worrying, and this remains one of the stubborn apartheid legacies to uproot. In such a situation, a bargaining democracy in which groups fend for themselves by disrupting the system will not be ideal. This seems to be the direction in which South Africa may be headed – a bargaining democracy.

As the ANC closes in on its last decade of political hegemony in a democratic South Africa, the party will have to survive in a politically fragmented society with high social and economic tensions. This entails having to survive across regions, with a declining national political influence. The ANC regions will have to adapt to the needs of their local citizens to survive as well, and still to dominate. Holds on regional power will determine an area's influence on the national outlook and leadership of the ANC, as is already beginning to happen. For example, the ANC has no political power hold in government in the Western Cape, so the ANC's Western Cape region has less influence on the national leadership of the party.

While the ANC's national leadership will attempt to centralise power in the state to extend the party's hegemony, political developments will push the ANC regions to become more federal and autonomous if regional leaders are to stay in power, reluctantly pushing the ANC towards reform from below. Unless a political party that seeks to mobilise political support from the centre is formed, political fragmentation and the shift towards political extremism and identity politics will continue. This will not collapse South Africa's liberal-democratic project, but it will make it more conflict-prone and retard progress in development.

South Africa's policy space will, in this regard, be dominated by court battles and arbitration between powerful key stakeholders, instead of being driven by consensus aimed at a win-win scenario for all. South Africa's policy discourse will be dominated by strong figures, and will drift further away from the people. This could be the picture in the medium term.

State capacity remains a major challenge for fostering development and delivering services. The weakness in state capacity – including, even, in relation to the state's capacity to ensure that the rule of law prevails – is also observed by the neighbouring countries in the region. For example, Botswana's government decided to enlist the services of AfriForum to prosecute, privately, alleged money-laundering offences in Botswana involving South African mining tycoon Bridgette Radebe. This makes it difficult for South Africa to persuade its peers in the region when it comes to ensuring that the rule of law is preserved.

Despite its declining public support in the past decade, and the likely loss of its absolute majority by 2029, the ANC will remain a political force to be reckoned with. However, it will have no choice but to adapt to the country's shifting political dynamics. That chapter of its long history remains to be written, but the party will likely resort to new strategies in a desperate attempt to continue its dominance over society.

The giant will not go quietly into the night.

Acknowledgements

First and foremost, I would like to thank my friend and publisher, Maryna Lamprecht, for her willingness to listen to my ideas and for our many stimulating conversations about the state of the nation's politics. My relationship with Maryna stretches back to her days as a political journalist, and has already given rise to three books.

As he sculpted my first draft, Albert Weideman amplified my voice masterfully. I am forever indebted to Albert for taking time from his demanding schedule to help with this project. I would also like to thank Angela Voges for her incredible editing skill as she sharpened the text further.

This project would not have happened without the support of Professor Chris Landsberg of the University of Johannesburg and the South African Research Chairs Initiative. He afforded me the space and financial support necessary to pursue the work I am passionate about. The staff in Professor Landsberg's office, Sandile Moloi and Yasmin Sibran, also provided patient support, for which I am deeply grateful.

To my good friend Mike Milazi, thanks for always being there to brainstorm ideas as we try to take the political pulse of the country. To Stephen Grootes, thank you for writing the foreword. Your name is synonymous with professionalism and integrity in political journalism, and I am honoured that it features on the pages of this book. I would also like to thank my fellow political junkie Jan-Jan

Joubert, who provided invaluable feedback after reading the manuscript.

To my parents, Solly and Constance, thanks for raising me in a stimulating environment where I was exposed to current affairs from an early age. Your love for debate and diversity of thought enrich my life to this very day.

Finally, my gratitude also goes to all the journalists with whom I engage on a daily basis. Without your input and your probing questions about political and social developments, my work would be immeasurably poorer.

Index

Abedian, Iraj 24
Abrahams, Shaun 185
accountability 13–16
affirmative action 11, 99, 204
African National Congress (ANC)
  branches of 13, 128–131
  coalitions and 133–134, 137–139
  democratic centralism 10–17, 124–126, 183, 185–187, 189
  economic growth and 62–75
  elections 8, 14, 38–48, 76, 84, 104–117, 118–131, 143, 159, 194, 199–201, 207–208
  elective conference in 2022 110, 116, 162–169, 170–180, 186–187
  factionalism 14–16, 18, 20–22, 25, 65, 111–112, 128, 181
  history of 5–17
  image of 39–48, 121–122, 125–126
  Integrity Commission 25–26, 173–174, 179
  local government and 76–90, 122–123, 207
  Mangaung conference (2012) 8, 25, 40–41, 177
  middle class and 157–161
  Morogoro Conference (1969) 10–11
  Nasrec conference (2017) 18–20, 64, 71, 73, 105, 111, 162, 167–168
  National Executive Committee 13, 19, 21, 22, 25–26, 52–53, 72, 124, 167, 177
  National Working Committee 21
  opposition parties and 91–93, 95–99, 101–103
  Polokwane conference (2007) 164
  rural areas and 123–124, 129, 143–152
  self-correction in 12, 27, 47, 109, 111
  SOEs and 49–53, 56–61
  Top Six 13, 19, 167–168, 170
African National Congress Youth League (ANCYL) 25, 176
AfriForum 190, 208
Afrobarometer 40
agriculture sector 68, 149
America see United States of America
ANC see African National Congress
ANCYL see African National Congress Youth League
anti-establishment politics 93, 94, 164, 169
apartheid 80, 127, 154
Aristotle 153–156
asbestos roof scandal 21, 34, 171
Auditor-General 79–80, 82, 84

Baloyi, Bongani 83–84
bargain democracy 197–198, 207
Barkhuizen, Elana 102
Batohi, Shamila 34, 183
BEE see black economic empowerment
Bell Pottinger 92–93
black economic empowerment (BEE) 11, 16, 99, 157, 204
Bloomberg News 55, 59
Bosasa 44–45
Botswana 208
Brown, Lynne 33
business sector 28–29, 66–70, 74, 111, 183

Cabinet after 2019 elections 22–25
cadre deployment 19, 27–29, 83
Capricorn District Municipality 82
Carnilinx 94
Cele, Bheki 23

centralisation of power 10–17, 83, 86–89, 122, 124–126, 128–131, 207
centre politics 102, 136, 203–207
City of Johannesburg 46, 84, 102–103, 138–139
City of Tshwane 84, 138–139
City Press 42
Coalition Country 123, 136–137
coalitions 84, 102–103, 116, 120–121, 128–129, 134–142, 187, 202
collective, emphasis on 11
collective responsibility 13–15
commissions of inquiry 34–35 *see also* Zondo Commission
compromise 120, 129, 137
Confederation of South African Trade Unions 55, 62, 69
consensus 187–189, 207
constituency system 77, 88–89, 114, 131, 148
Constitutional Court 78–79, 89, 91, 113–114, 192–193
Constitution of South Africa 11, 17, 80, 87–89, 132, 190–191, 194–196, 204
consultative decision-making 80–81, 124–125, 140–142, 183–187
corporate sector *see* business sector
corruption
　ANC and 64–65, 72, 105–106, 108–113, 134, 158, 174–176, 204
　bureaucratic system against 193–194
　EFF and 93, 96–98
　impact of 41–43
　in local government 79–80, 86
　privatisation and 46
　Ramaphosa and 26–27, 39–40, 43, 63, 108–112, 164–169, 181–182
　in SOEs 50–52
Cosatu see Confederation of South African Trade Unions
courts 193, 195–197
COVID-19 pandemic 39–40, 52–53, 55–56, 60, 65, 70–73, 174–176, 178

DA *see* Democratic Alliance
Dahl, Robert 133
Daily Maverick 24
debt 65, 71
decentralisation 129–131, 193–194
decision-making process 7, 10–17, 124–125, 141–142, 183–187, 196
De Lille, Patricia 121–122
democracy 46, 132–133, 153–157
Democratic Alliance (DA) 8, 39, 82–86, 90–92, 97–103, 115, 119, 121–122, 125–126, 134–137, 144, 159–160, 170, 174, 188, 197, 201–205
democratic centralism 10–17, 124–126, 183, 185–187, 189
Denel 42, 49, 51, 54
Department of Mineral Resources and Energy 57, 58–59
Department of Public Enterprises 32–33, 54–55, 57
De Ruyter, André 33
developmental states 201
dictatorship 186, 201
direct representation 76–78, 79
District Development Model 85–89, 200–201
Dlamini-Zuma, Nkosazana 18, 162, 167–168
Dlodlo, Ayanda 23
Duarte, Jessie 19, 47, 108, 159, 167, 176
Dube, John Langalibalele 9

Eastern Cape 119, 143, 176
Economic Freedom Fighters (EFF) 25, 44, 61, 91–98, 102–103, 115, 137–139, 144, 159, 170, 187–188, 197, 201–202, 204–205
economic growth 46–47, 53, 62–75, 149, 151–152, 166
Eddins, Berkley 10
education 158–159, 196
EFF *see* Economic Freedom Fighters
elections 8, 14, 38–48, 76–77, 84, 97, 99–117, 118–131, 132–134, 138–140, 143–144, 159, 164–166, 169, 172, 181–183, 186–187, 202
electoral reform 76–79, 114–115, 129–130, 191–193
electricity 49–50, 57–60, 67
elite groups 9, 12–13, 139–140

Ellis, Stephen 9, 11, 12
eNCA 38
EOH Holdings 179
Equal Education 196
Eskom 32–33, 43, 49–51, 54, 57–60, 69, 174
ethnicity 127, 137, 150–151
e-tolls 130
executive leadership 187–189
expropriation of land without compensation 64, 150, 157, 195

factionalism 14–16, 18, 20–22, 25, 65, 111–112, 128, 181
failed state, South Africa as 197–198
Fakir, Ebrahim 78
farming *see* agriculture sector
farm murders 100–101, 136
federalism 83, 87, 117, 125–127, 129, 152, 207
finance minister position 23, 31–32
financial cluster (Cabinet) 22–23, 30, 31
Freedom Front Plus 135
Free State 119, 131
Frolick, Cedric 45
Fukuyama, Francis 205–206
funding 112–114
Future Tense 202–203

Gangster State 171
Gauteng 119–120, 127, 130, 143, 175–176
Gebrekidan, Selam 173
Gigaba, Malusi 32, 179
Gordhan, Pravin 23, 31–32, 33, 54–58, 93–94
government institutions 14, 19–20, 27–36, 163, 200–201 *see also* state-owned enterprises
Gramsci, Antonio 199–200
Gumede, William 78
Gupta family 16, 28, 51

health sector 72, 175–176 *see also* COVID-19 pandemic
hegemony 199–201, 207
Hlabisa, Velenkosini 170
How to Steal a City 82
Huntington, Samuel 45–46

Identity 205–206
identity politics 85, 100–101, 102, 136, 188, 205–207
IFP *see* Inkatha Freedom Party
IMF *see* International Monetary Fund
Inclusive Society Institute 78
Independent Electoral Commission 43–44
independent panels of inquiry 34–36, 54, 183–185
independent parliamentary candidates 114–115, 148
industrial policy 67–68
inequality 64, 94, 97, 206–207
Inkatha Freedom Party (IFP) 151, 170
International Monetary Fund (IMF) 73

Jiba, Nomgcobo 34, 185
Johannesburg *see* City of Johannesburg
Jonas, Mcebisi 29, 31
judiciary 96, 108, 169, 195–196

Kathrada, Ahmed 26
Kgetlengrivier Local Municipality 42
Kieswetter, Edward 30
Kingon, Mark 30
Kodwa, Zizi 179
KwaZulu-Natal 119, 127, 151, 176

Lamola, Ronald 177
Landman, JP 36
land reform policy 11, 64, 68, 149–150, 157, 195, 201
leadership styles 182–189
Leon, Tony 202–203
liberalism 11, 46, 101, 132–133, 203–206
liberation parties 14–15, 104, 109, 200
Limpopo 118, 144, 151, 176
load shedding 49, 60
local government 41–43, 76–90, 115, 122–123, 144–148
Lodge, Tom 46, 124–125
looting of public resources 16–17, 33, 39–40, 81

Mabuza, David 19, 162, 167–168, 172–174
Magashule, Ace 19–21, 26, 34, 98, 163–164, 167, 171–172, 174, 181

Mahumapelo, Supra 26–27, 163, 164, 174
Maimane, Mmusi 99–101, 102, 160, 202–203
Makhura, David 175–176
Makwetu, Kimi 79
Malawi 14, 103, 133
Malema, Julius 93–98, 138, 170, 177
Mandela, Nelson 15, 47
Mantashe, Gwede 19, 26, 57–59, 167, 176
Manuel, Trevor 31
Mapisa-Nqakula, Nosiviwe 23
Mashaba, Herman 89–90, 100, 160
Mashamaite, Tlhalefi 79–80
Mashatile, Paul 19, 167, 170, 175–176
Mashinini, Glen 43
Masuku, Bandile 175
Mathabatha, Stanley 22
Matjila, Dan 35
Mazibuko, Lindiwe 102, 160
Mazzotti, Adriano 94
Mbalula, Fikile 179
Mbeki, Thabo 31, 172, 196
Mboweni, Tito 23, 31–32, 56–57, 62, 69–70, 73, 98, 165–166
Mchunu, Senzo 19
media 38, 40–41, 47–48
Meyer, Roelf 78
middle class 153–161, 182, 188
Midvaal municipality 84
Mkhwebane, Busisiwe 93
Mlangeni, Andrew 26
Modise, Thandi 44
Mogalakwena Municipality 79–80
Mokgoro, Yvonne 34
Molefe, Brian 32
Moody's 65, 71
Motlanthe, Kgalema 171
Motsepe, Patrice 32
Motsoaledi, Aaron 77–78
Moyane, Tom 30, 35
Mpati, Lex 35
Mphithi, Luyolo 101–102
Mpumalanga 119, 173–174
Mrwebi, Lawrence 34, 185
Mufamadi, Sydney 44
municipalities see local government; service delivery

Myburgh, Pieter-Louis 171
Myeni, Dudu 31, 50

National Development Plan 68
National Executive Committee (NEC) 13, 19, 21, 22, 25–26, 52–53, 72, 124, 167, 177
nationalisation of Reserve Bank 64, 70, 71
nationalism 198, 205, 206
National Prosecuting Authority (NPA) 24, 27, 33–34, 163–164, 183, 184–185
National Treasury 30–32, 62–63, 66–70, 166
Ndabeni-Abrahams, Stella 178
NEC see National Executive Committee
Nelson Mandela Bay Metro 82, 84, 138
Nene, Nhlanhla 23, 31–32
nepotism 42, 79, 166–167
New Nation case 78–79, 89, 114–115, 191–193
New Nation Movement 114, 191–193
News24 136
New York Times, The 173
NGOs see non-governmental organisations
Nkandla homestead 91, 96
Nkoana-Mashabane, Maite 24
non-governmental organisations (NGOs) 191, 193–196
Northern Cape 119, 143
North West 119
NPA see National Prosecuting Authority
Nt'sekhe, Refiloe 102
Nugent Commission of Inquiry 35
Nupen, Dren 78
Nxasana, Mxolisi 185
Nxesi, Thulas 24

Olver, Crispian 82
Onishi, Norimitsu 173
opposition parties 14, 40, 76, 91–103, 107, 119, 133, 144, 146–147, 196–197, 201

Parliament 44–45, 77, 195
patronage 13, 28–29, 33, 42–43, 46, 128
PIC see Public Investment Corporation

policy issues 11–12, 18, 21–22, 63–75, 120, 132–134, 140–142, 150–151, 157, 193–196, 203–204, 207
political fragmentation 123, 188–189, 194, 196–197, 204–207
political identities 125–127, 137, 194
Politics (Aristotle) 153–156
poverty 64, 94, 97, 148–149, 154–157, 191
power 2–3
privatisation 46, 51–55, 61
property rights 157, 195
proportional representation 76, 78, 79
protests 40, 43–44, 81–82
provincial sphere of government 86–88, 116–126, 128–131
Przeworski, Adam 156
Public Investment Corporation (PIC) 35
Public Protector 91, 93, 171
public-sector wage bill 63–64, 66, 71, 73, 84 *see also* salaries, failing to pay

race 99–102, 136–137, 154, 160, 202–205
Radebe, Bridgette 208
radical economic transformation (RET) 64–65, 71, 74, 92, 168
radical economic transformation (RET) faction (Zuma faction) 18–23, 26–27, 36, 42, 73, 105, 109, 111–112, 162–169, 174, 181, 186
Ramaphosa, Cyril
  age of 170
  corruption and 26–27, 39–40, 43, 63, 108–112, 164–169, 181–182
  economic growth and 32–33, 62–64, 66–75, 166
  election results and 105–108, 182–183
  elective conference in 2022 116, 162–171, 177–179
  faction 15–16, 18–22, 168–169, 176
  independent panels of inquiry 34–36, 54, 183–185
  leadership style of 18–37, 182–186
  legacy of 181–189
  local government and 85
  opposition parties and 92–93
  SOEs and 51, 53–54, 56, 58–61
Ratanang Trust 96

rating agencies *see* sovereign rating agencies
real estate development 149–150
red tape, new businesses 62, 67
Reserve Bank 31, 63, 64, 70, 71
RET *see* radical economic transformation
Reuters 68
rule of law 111, 196, 208
rural areas 81, 123–124, 129, 143–152

SAA *see* South African Airways
SABC *see* South African Broadcasting Corporation
SACP *see* South African Communist Party
salaries, failing to pay 42, 51, 60 *see also* public-sector wage bill
SALDRU *see* Southern Africa Labour and Development Research Unit
SARS *see* South African Revenue Service
Schreiber, Leon 123, 136–137
security, private 158
security cluster (Cabinet) 23–24
service delivery 19, 40–43, 79–81, 131, 140–141, 144–148, 157–158, 195, 197, 208
Shilowa, Mbhazima 176
Shivambu, Floyd 95, 97, 170
Simelane, Menzi 24, 185
Simkins, Charles 203
Sisulu, Lindiwe 179
Slabbert, Frederick van Zyl 78
small and medium businesses 67
Smith, Vincent 44
social grants 145
social media 39–40, 98–99, 163
SOEs *see* state-owned enterprises
South African Airways (SAA) 31–33, 49–57, 60, 69–70
South African Broadcasting Corporation (SABC) 72
South African Communist Party (SACP) 12, 55, 62, 69
South African Municipal Workers' Union 42

South African Reserve Bank *see* Reserve Bank
South African Revenue Service (SARS) 27, 29–31, 35, 93–94, 163
Southall, Roger 53
Southern Africa Labour and Development Research Unit (SALDRU) 155
sovereign rating agencies 65, 70, 71
Special Investigating Unit 39–40
state capture 19, 50–55, 64–65, 106, 134, 194–195
state institutions *see* government institutions
State of the Nation address (2021) 165
state-owned enterprises (SOEs) 32–33, 49–61, 69–70, 72 *see also* government institutions
Statistics South Africa 63
Steenhuisen, John 100, 135, 170
subsistence economy 152

Tarr, Alan 126, 127
telecommunications sector 67, 69
title deeds 149–150, 152
trade unions 56, 59, 61, 74
traditional leadership authorities 144, 146–150
transformation project 11, 15–16, 53, 194, 203–205
Transnet 49, 54
Treasury *see* National Treasury
Truman, Harry 13
Tshwane *see* City of Tshwane
Twitter 99, 163

unemployment 63–64, 68, 72
unions *see* trade unions

United States of America (USA) 126–127, 143
Universal Service and Access Agency of South Africa (Usaasa) 178
urbanisation 145, 150, 152
USA *see* United States of America
Usaasa *see* Universal Service and Access Agency of South Africa

Van Rooyen, Des 23, 31–32
VBS Mutual Bank 95–96, 97

wages *see* public sector wage bill; salaries, failing to pay
Western Cape 119, 121–122, 125–126, 135, 207
white minority 99, 100, 135–137, 154
white monopoly capital 64, 92–93, 168
World Bank 63

younger leaders 88, 112, 170, 177–180
young people 25, 43–45, 63–64, 97, 110, 112

Zikalala, Sihle 178–179
Zille, Helen 99–100, 102, 121–122, 135, 159–160
Zimbabwe 104
Zondo Commission 19, 26, 44, 50–51, 77, 96–97, 108, 113, 179
Zuma, Jacob 21, 23–24, 28, 31–33, 47, 50, 91–92, 95–96, 101, 107–108, 119, 130, 158–159, 164, 170–172, 184–185
Zuma era 16–17, 19, 25–26, 28–34, 50, 64, 92, 134
Zuma faction (RET faction) 18–23, 26–27, 36, 42, 73, 105, 109, 111–112, 162–169, 174, 181, 186

RALPH MATHEKGA is a South African author and one of the country's leading political analysts and columnists. His first book, *When Zuma Goes*, was published in 2016, and his second book, *Ramaphosa's Turn: Can Cyril Save South Africa?* in 2018.

He has taught politics at the University of the Western Cape and worked as a senior policy analyst at the National Treasury. He is often quoted by both local and international media, and he comments regularly on television and radio.

Ralph has a PhD in politics and is currently a postdoctoral research fellow with the South African Research Chairs Initiative (SARChI): African Diplomacy and Foreign Policy at the University of Johannesburg.